Costume Design for
Video Games

Costume Design for Video Games

An Exploration of Historical and Fantastical Skins

Edited by

Sandy Appleoff Lyons

CRC Press
Taylor & Francis Group
Boca Raton London New York

CRC Press is an imprint of the
Taylor & Francis Group, an **informa** business

CRC Press
Taylor & Francis Group
6000 Broken Sound Parkway NW, Suite 300
Boca Raton, FL 33487-2742

© 2020 by Taylor & Francis Group, LLC
CRC Press is an imprint of Taylor & Francis Group, an Informa business

No claim to original U.S. Government works

Printed on acid-free paper

International Standard Book Number-13: 978-1-138-08605-0 (Hardback)
International Standard Book Number-13: 978-1-138-08596-1 (Paperback)

Visit the Taylor & Francis Web site at
http://www.taylorandfrancis.com

and the CRC Press Web site at
http://www.crcpress.com

Contents

Acknowledgments

It is hard to believe 13 years have passed since I crafted out the curriculum for the Game Art Major at Laguna College of Art and Design. At that time, having come from an MFA in scenography, costume, stage, and lighting design, I saw direct correlations between building virtual worlds and the tactile illusionary worlds created on the stage. It was in 2006 that I began my journey into the world of game production.

As any teacher worth their salt knows, you get back what you put into a class, which means that teaching is a give and receive process. I have learned as much, and most likely more, from my colleagues and my students as I ever learned in school or on the job in the arts industry.

As the Game Art BFA piloted out, it was blessed first with strong existing majors that comprised Laguna College of Art and Design. They became the backbone on which the major was built.

The neighboring professional community in game opened their arms to the major and not only provided the largest learning curve I have ever tried to tackle in a short amount of time but also led me to some of the most inspirational, talented, kind, caring, and motivated people I have been blessed to know.

Lastly but not least, my thanks to my students, the early ones, to those who felt the growing pains of a new major, but survived and are now part of a thriving industry in game. And the students later on, that came into a solidly developed major with all-star faculty. It is their work I am honored to be sharing with you.

For those who have contributed to the written portion of the book, first let me say thank you to Jaime Stagg, whose kind smile could completely change the demeanor of a classroom and whose work was an inspiration to those around her. Jaime's contribution to this book is in Chapter 8.

And Anna Sakoi: her quiet demeanor honored her precision and excellence in execution of any project she undertook. She is a tribute to those who lead by deed and not word. Anna's contribution to this book is in Chapter 8.

And a very special thanks to all of the students whose work is showcased in the book.

Thank you to Jennifer Martinez Wormser, another beautiful woman, who could instantly change your day with her positive spirit. Jennifer's contribution to the research for the Art of Costume class helped to hone the classes' research skills. Jennifer's contribution is in Chapter 7.

To my colleague and good friend, Lou Police, I will always be eternally grateful for his thoughtful gifts of support and grace. Lou is a master; Lou's contribution is in Chapter 3.

And to whom this book is dedicated, Gavin Rich, my friend, my colleague, my mentor, and at times now my boss. I could never have done any of this without you, Gavin. You will find Gavin's contribution in Chapter 1.

Coming from a linage of teachers, I would like to thank another teacher from my family, my cousin, Marcia Schwartz – published author, retired English teacher, and an eagle eye for grammar details. Marcia polished for all of us, as I nervously prepared the book for submission.

I hope you find value in this information and gain mastery to enhance your own system of research and problem-solving, as it relates to costume design for games and films.

Introduction

I remember at a young age sitting around the dinner table with my parents and their friends, one of which was the president of a local college, talking about how we processed and retained information in learning. The visual, audio, and kinetic trio (or combination of one, two, or all three) left me analyzing classes I slept through, classes I excelled at, and every class I ever taught. The pedagogy behind the structure of the Art of Costume class was developed while I was chairing the undergraduate major in Game Art at Laguna College of Art and Design (LCAD). It was a thoughtful journey down the combination of all opportunities to create value in the class materials for retention and the development of a creative problem-solving process that would adapt itself to each student's personal rate of learning.

In my undergraduate program, I ended up practically cross-eyed working in the microfiche library at the University of Kansas searching down information that is now at our fingertips. We are now becoming more and more symbiotic with our computer tools. As a result, we rely on those tools to remember facts for us. So we then create a new line of connectivity or new relationships to process information. Technology will enhance your research skills, but it cannot replace creative problem-solving or fundamental drawing and design skills. Your challenge is to hone your mind (and problem-solving skills) to be as strong as your drawing, design, and research skills.

> A technology-based, closed-loop approach can be used to generate an experience that activates brain networks in a selective manner (that's how the brain works) and then applies constant pressure to the network via interactive challenges that drive the brain's plasticity to optimize its function over time.
>
> *The Cognition Crisis by Adam Gazzaley MD, PhD*

It is my belief that our kinetic to visual information gathering is one of the best means of retaining information. If you draw it, you remember it. There are many learning styles, and it is my hope that I will motivate yours. Having evolved into a quick information society, we tend to not retain what we learn as our brains opt to utilize secondary devices for storage. This can be an advantage and/or an extreme disadvantage when designing. Building context for designs via style sheets, style bibles, and style guides gives us groundwork to immerse ourselves into real and imaginary realms so as to create the suspension of disbelief. One of the goals of this book is to give you the foundational overview of Western cultural clothing from the Mesopotamians to the Northern Renaissance via a story-driven narrative. This, in turn, gives you context to draw upon for your designs.

In historically-inspired costume design, we are constantly looking for analogies, similarities, and differences. The end goal is the birth of another creative problem-solving process or way of learning the skill for ourselves. As a student of this skill set, you need to be able to solve unstructured problems with new and old research and information available to you, and then pepper it with your own style.

If you really want to gain and keep the expertise in this area or skill set, you need to find a way to make it personally meaningful. I believe, if we can make it deeply meaningful, then you will be far more capable of recalling the history and methodology put forth in this book.

In the classroom I have often used Howard Pyle's quote, "throw your heart into your work, and then jump in after it." If you are going to spend time doing this, do it better than you have ever done anything before. Master it, own it, make it yours. The more effort you put forth, the more you gain.

Our imaginations are such an important tool to keep alive. Each of us has systems we use in the creative process, or ways we go about solving a design problem. I will have you engage in one process, which I call the "Immortal," which we will use as a learning tool as we travel time and explore cross-cultural design. The "Immortal" is the character in our story, the personality that makes choices, the short, tall, skinny, part alien, big-bottomed, purple polka-dotted immortal that is personal in such a way that the student could identify with the story or character development around it. You, the student, are the puppet master, pulling the strings of our immortal character and interweaving your historical costume history with new authentic costume designs that are not impeded by time (Figure 0.1).

As a class or a self-study book, we want to develop your understanding of historical costumes, improve your research skills beyond an internet search, and give you a methodology you can use to develop your own process. This is a process for creating historically-based costume designs and original designs based on the cross-pollination of two cultures. The end product being beyond the understanding of historical context in costume will be the ability to then convey the knowledge gained by creating style sheets, character layout sheets, and production tools that are easily understood and visually impactful, and show

Figure 0.1

Example "Immortal" (Veronica Liwski)

that you are capable of thinking around a design in all of its detail to be a vital part of the production process in games, real and extended reality, or any other entertainment medium utilizing characters.

The process of drawing style sheets, or kinetic and visual input, for each historical chapter helps to store the information in our long-term memory. The mind–body connection is a real one, and those of you that have spent years drawing know that muscle memory does exist in relationship to your drawing skills.

Let's start by breaking it down in learnable components, thus managing the cognitive load.

The book is subdivided into informative chapters, how-to chapters, and historical chapters.

The informative chapters/inserts stand alone. They are content to consider to provide general knowledge about the creative pipeline.

The "how-to" chapters are supportive material to fine-tune the skill sets, and provide knowledge of the process that is needed for creating a successful industry-ready end product.

The historical chapters are designed to be learning tools in costume history, character development, and the understanding of the cultural and technological advancements that made an impact on costume or clothing of the time.

I created two Immortals whose storylines will help you to understand the development of a character while taking you through time. Understanding the character that you are clothing in relationship to the world and time in which he/she is existing is important in creating the believable suspension of disbelief. Within the narrative asides, I have created callouts specific to the costume of the time. You will find me using "callouts" quite often in the book and in reference to the style sheets you hopefully will be creating. Within those callouts are the illustrations from my students in the Art of Costume class at LCAD from 2008 to present, most of which came from the style sheets they created each week (Figure 0.2).

Figure 0.2

Example style sheet (Sarah Pan).

My challenge to you is to structure a sheet to work with each historical chapter of the book. This in turn will help you to understand the history behind the costume of the time and imprint it upon your memory by kinetically drawing the information you need to know. In working with art directors, art teams, modelers, or producers, your ability to convey a multitude of information at a glance is one very good skill set. Even better yet is to be able to carry on a conversation about the period of time in relationship to the costume you are designing. If memory fails you, you then have a time capsule or a visual diary at your fingertips.

Editor

Sandy Appleoff Lyons was born and raised in Falls City, Nebraska, where she currently lives with her husband Tim and her chocolate lab, Coco Chanel.

Starting in 1983 Sandy began her teaching career with a Fashion Illustration course taught at the Kansas City Art Institute, while working full time for Hallmark Cards. Education soon became the passion in her professional career as her desire moved to engaging and inspiring young learners on to fulfilling careers.

Sandy's graduate degree was in costume, stage, and lighting design for the theatre (Scenography) at the University of Kansas. Her background soon moved from the stage to the virtual worlds of game design, where today she chairs the Game Design MFA at Laguna College of Art and Design.

Contributors

Lou Police graduated from ArtCenter College of Design LA, Pasadena, California, in 1978 with a BFA in Illustration. His most influential instructors are Harry Carmean, Gregory Weir-Quiton, Vern Wilson, Kathy Wirch, Ward Kimball, Herb Ryman, and John Asaro.

His freelance illustration assignments include movie poster designs, book illustration, magazine illustration, advertising storyboarding and comps, fashion illustration, matte painting, and live action production art. His clients include Tony Seiniger, TV Guide, The LA Times, ILM, and Introvision Systems.

Animation companies he has worked for are Ralph Bakshi Animation, Richard Williams Animation in Los Angeles, DIC, Warner Bros. Television, Warner Bros. Feature, Walt Disney Television, Disney Toon Studios, Walt Disney Feature, and Fox. His responsibilities at these companies included character design, background design, background painting, storyboarding, visual development, and art direction.

His teaching experience includes ArtCenter College of Design, Cal Arts, Laguna College of Art and Design, Woodbury University, and The Fashion Institute of Los Angeles. His Western-themed fine art gallery work was represented by Trailside Galleries in Scottsdale, Arizona, and Jackson Hole, Wyoming. He is currently teaching at ArtCenter College of Design in Pasadena and Laguna College of Art and Design in Laguna Beach.

Gavin Rich is an artist, designer, and instructor for games. He has been working in the gaming industry for 15 years on projects ranging from AAA action games to cute mobile projects. While Gavin started his career focusing on concept and character modeling, he quickly fell in love with the whole development process. This passion drove him to go back to get his MFA in Game Design at Laguna College of Art+Design (LCAD) to help realize his own projects.

Currently, Gavin is the chair of the Game Art Department at LCAD where he gets to help create his favorite artists. Growing up in the redwoods of Northern California has given Gavin a love of nature and hope for a positive future that can be seen throughout his work. His most recent project is about a robot cleaning up park trails.

Anna Sakoi is the Lead 3D Artist at Super Evil Megacorp where she works on the heroes and creatures of *Vainglory*. She received her BFA in Game Art with a minor in Sculpture from Laguna College of Art and Design in 2014. Besides working on video game characters, she also dabbles in 3D printing and traditional sculpture on the side. When not working on art, she likes to spend time with her pet cats and rabbits. You can find her portfolio at www.artstation.com/annasakoi.

Jaime Stagg works out of her home studio in Irvine, California, as a freelance 3D designer working for Hasbro. She graduated from Laguna College of Art and Design (LCAD) in 2014 with a degree in Game Art with emphasis on 3D character and a minor in Sculpture. Jaime has a bronze statue in LCAD's permanent collection and has shown her work in the Juried Student exhibition in 2014, as well as the uBe Art Gallery in Berkeley. She has a passion for designer toys, sculpture, and costumes. Aside from art, she enjoys traveling, practicing to make the best cup of matcha, and playing with her dog, Mika.

Jennifer Martinez Wormser is the library director at the Ella Strong Denison Library at Scripps College. Prior to accepting her current position, she was the library director at the Laguna College of Art and Design for nine years and has worked with manuscript and archival materials at UCLA, San Diego State University, the Huntington Library, and the Sherman Library & Gardens. She was elected as the President of the Society of California Archivists in 2004–2005, served on the California Historical Resources Advisory Board from 2005 to 2010, taught a course on archives for San Jose State University's Graduate School of Library and Information Science from 2006 to 2009, and also developed and taught a class at Laguna College of Art and Design on the art and history of the book. In 2017, she was part of a team of librarians who received the Worldwide Books Award for Electronic Resources from the Art Libraries Society of North America (ARLIS/NA) for their development of the *lynda.com* tutorial, *Information Literacy with Elsa Loftis*. She has a BA in English from Scripps College and an MLS degree with a concentration in archival management from the University of Maryland, College Park.

1

Pipeline Costumes for Games

Gavin Rich

Costumes communicate a character's intent in games. Is this character good? Is he, she, or it bad? Is this someone capable of betrayal later in the story? Is he an adventurer? Is she a soldier?

These story elements can be hinted at through subtle elements in the character's design, and great care should be taken when designing key nonplayer characters. What about the players themselves though, and how do you make costumes that are going to evolve with the players' growth in the game or help them display their personality in the world? Character customization has become a key component in games and has changed the way characters are thought about in production. Villagers can be randomly generated from a suite of outfits; bandits can each feel like they have their own style and their own story by mixing and matching outfits together. Making a system like this work takes some planning, and creating all of the assets can take loads of human power, but if done well, it can create an immersive world that players will love.

There are two camps when it comes to character customization: one is "GIVE THEM FULL CONTROL I WANT THEM TO GET WEIRD", and the other is "I want these characters to always feel like they belong in the world, any combo should feel designed". I fall into the second group so this chapter will be focusing on the second technique. That does not dismiss the first method, however; I love playing games that have the fidelity to make Marge Simpson or Christopher Walken from the same customization screen. A chapter about full customization would be much more at home in a book about programming though, not one about visual design.

Setting up a strong character customization pipeline should be thought of the same way you decide what to wear in the morning. Design is all about asking the right questions about the intent of the task. I was once told by a mentor that "every morning is a practice in character design".

Am I going to work?
Am I lounging around home?
Am I going out with friends?
Am I going to a wedding?

All of these outfits are in your closet, but you will not wear your work clothes to a wedding, and you will not wear your lounge around home sweats when you go to work. We all have intuition on what to ask; we just need to dig deep on the intent of the design. Some common questions to ask when designing character outfit ideas follow the same ideas in our own outfit choices.

What is the primary task the player performs?
Does this outfit help with gameplay?
Is this outfit just for aesthetics?
What is the fantasy this outfit fulfills?
Does this outfit represent a milestone the character has achieved?
Does this outfit represent an area of the world?

There are many more questions to ask, but these are a great place to start.

Okay, we have our answers so we know the type of outfits we need for the character: now it is time to start designing.

Our first step is to define our limitations. What kind of technical support is on the character customization? If there is a dedicated programmer or two on the project, you will have a lot more range in what you can accomplish. I will stay simple for this to focus on a majority of use cases. Most games are going to have three or four pieces to customize. The hat, the coat, and the pants are the primary pieces to swap out. Sometimes pants and boots are separated; sometimes they go together. This setup makes it easier on the tech end but can still give some hard problems to navigate for the art team. Can we have long coats that go past the beltline? If we do, does that mean we can't have bulky belt pieces? You come to a point where you have to make some hard decisions on what can be used in designs and what cannot be used in designs. If done right, players won't notice that you are working around limitations. If done wrong, however, you end up with meshes that feel like they are puffy and floating over the body just in case the mesh underneath has extra pieces that stick out further than the agreed-upon distance. Instead of designing around constraints and sticking to limitations, you are forced to problem solve around worst-case scenarios, and the character starts to lose his or her believability. Get the team on board early on, and don't stray from the constraints unless there is a technical solution that makes it viable.

Once we have our design constraints, we can start building. There are three tips that I will focus on that make life easier throughout this process:

1. The first tip is to create volumes or cages around each section of the body that is customizable. This volume represents the maximum distance a piece of the costume can extrude. Anything past this point and animations will cause pieces to clip together. Having these volumes gives the animators something to work with early in production so they can get a head start on their work.

2. The second tip is to have some sort of proxy mesh that each piece can snap to so you know the intersections will always line up. Some studios use a spline and some use a mesh, just make sure that the edges snap to that line so shirts that look tucked in always have the pants line where they appear to insert. Personally, I like to have my base human mesh broken up by color. Each colored section represents a type of clothing – pants, shirts, boots, gloves. I break the colors at polygon edges so I can snap to that line later on and I know everything will fit together.

3. The third tip is to set up a base mesh with morph targets to transfer an outfit to different body types. Sculpting and altering a mesh to each of the body types within your game will allow you to cycle through each body type using a morph target system rather than trying to alter them by hand. This process can be made into a batch system so you can just hit a button and have it automated for you. With this, I normally build to the medium body type to give the least amount of distortion when stretching and shrinking the character's proportions.

Once these are set up, you can start the process of actually creating the clothes. While ZBrush will still be used heavily throughout the process, a new program has made a big splash in the past five years, Marvelous Designer. Marvelous Designer has an amazing system that allows artists to create clothing digitally, the same way they would be designed traditionally. Since the program was intended for the fashion industry, Marvelous Designer yields great results. The program has created a bridge where traditional costume designers can work in digital formats, and digital artists can create costumes that can be made in the real world.

To start, let's make a clothing set that has three shirts and three pairs of pants. First I need to define my constraints. To design is to work within constraints; don't just start making what you think is cool.

My game will be themed around people hiking in modern day.

My color palette will be geared towards classic outdoor wear – plaids, jeans, vests, jackets. Later I might make a set that would come from a climbing store or from a sports shop. Having these different themes allows the players to show where they have been in the game or to identify with different groups in the world.

I have decided that while a shirt can be tucked in, it is more likely to hang over the belt. With this decision, I am also limiting what can be on the belt. If anything is on the belt, it must not raise above the surface more than an inch so the shirt or jacket will not be clipped by it. Sorry hip pouch, none of you in this game.

Next, copy the section of the base mesh that represents the pants three times. I often move them to the side so I can see them all at once. Do the same for the shirts, and you should have three sets of the same copies of the body.

If there are any extra pieces I may need for my outfits, I block them out at this point. It is better to block out as much as you can, as simply as you can, early on so you have a good visual of what needs to be finished. I'm going to make one of my tops a shirt, one a jacket, and one a jacket with a vest. For the bottoms I will have jeans with sneakers, work pants with boots, and jeans with boots. I block out the meshes and change the base colors to match my palette and concepts.

This is where I would normally take things into ZBrush. I keep my base mesh and my cage in ZBrush so I can always check if my belt line is matching up and my pieces aren't going to clip when animating. If you are working with your clothing set in the same ZBrush file, you can toggle them on and off to try different costume pairings together. Always remember to keep checking how the outfits work together, if they are lined up on the connection lines, if they are clipping the base mesh, and if they are within the distance cage.

I'm not going to go into the pipeline of building a game-ready model so let's skip ahead.

Once we have our costume assets, we will say that the players can change the body type of their character. I will bring my base mesh into ZBrush and sculpt it into the different body types that I need. I can then reimport these models to be referenced as blend meshes. My original base mesh can reference these new shapes, and I can change its shape into these new forms.

Next, select all of your costume assets and skin or bind them to the base mesh. Now, when we change our blend shapes, we can see that the costume meshes change with the base mesh. We can automate this process, but always make sure you check your work. Sometimes this can have undesired effects on your meshes, and you will have to go in and warp sections by hand.

Using that same process, we can rig the base mesh and project its information over to our costume assets so we don't have to rig each one individually and we know each one will be matched to the base mesh.

There you have it; we now have a clothing set for a game character that we can switch around. Experiment with different ideas that were discussed here. What if you want to add a scarf? How do gloves come into play? What if you made the boots separate? You can turn the fidelity up or down as much as you want. You can have objects change shape depending on what has been equipped in different slots. The sky's the limit. Have fun with what you are doing and focus on making engaging characters that tell a story with their garments, and the player will embrace them.

2

Style Sheets

Sandy Appleoff Lyons

Sarah Pan

Each historical chapter we dive into will be accompanied by a terms list and examples of clothing of the era. The sketches used to exemplify the costume components were done by students at Laguna College of Art and Design. All of their sketches were done from authentic research of the period. If you are in a costume class quite possibly, the instructor is sharing actual period pieces with you. If you are going this on your own, you will need to really dig in and research period-authentic clothing to support the information provided in this book.

At the end of each historical chapter, I require my students, and urge you, to create a style sheet for that period. In the class we sketch from a model in period-authentic dress, and those sketches become the focal point of each style sheet (Figures 2.1 and 2.2).

I can't say it enough, drawing from life is a reinforcement for creating muscle memory for good drawing skills and creating a kinetic retention to the costume you are drawing. You will find that you can easily retain the specifics of the period costume if you have spent the time eye to hand, documenting it by sketching. It is a neural connect that no amount of computer research can give you. Even if you load up an existing piece of research and redraw it over the piece, it will give you better recall memory than if you just view it (Figure 2.3).

Figure 2.1

Photo of Costume by Christina Forst Modeled by Christina Forst.

Figure 2.2

Photo of Tim Forst.

Figure 2.3

Donna Vu

Style sheets are of particular importance in this class. Style guides or style sheets are used throughout the entertainment, edutainment, and any industry creating a specific style for an end project. The goal of a guide is to provide enough information to be able to pass on the project to another team member or client so they have the information needed to understand the nuances and are able to decipher the details that define that period or style.

The layout or design of a guide is a composition in its own right. It is the ability to creatively convey the information in a visually appealing way to sell your idea. It also shows your understanding of the materials, which is imperative. The ability to discuss period style with an art director or creative director is a strong asset to have.

For this module as we create a style guide layout for each period, I ask that you include the following in your style sheets:

1. Examples of both male and female dressed in period-correct costume (Figure 2.4).
2. Use one of the figures as your focal point and show both front and back views of the costume you have chosen to represent the period in detail. Provide enough information so that a three-dimensional (3D) artist can look at your drawing and model from it (Figure 2.5).
3. Do your best to represent the materials used for the costume and include callouts to support your drawings (Figure 2.6).

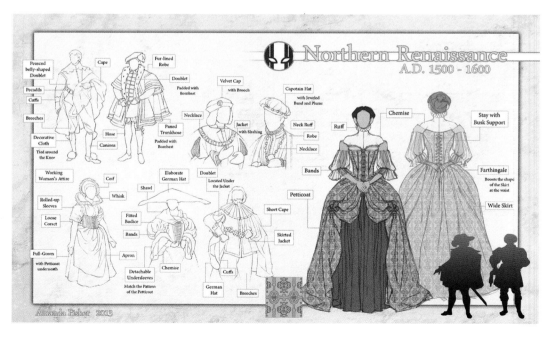

Figure 2.4

Amanda Fisher

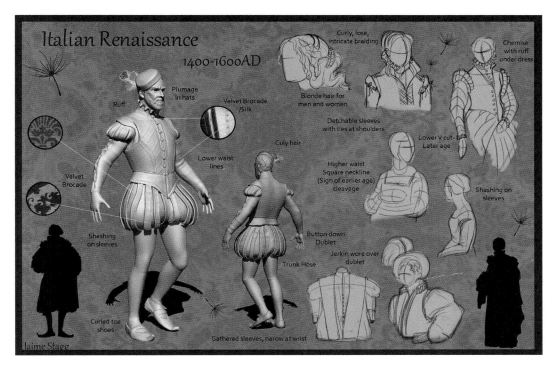

Figure 2.5

Jaime Stagg

Figure 2.6

Miranda Crowell

4. Draw each component of the costume and additional accessories that might be options for the time period (Figure 2.7).
5. Label everything! This is where the terms list comes in. Try to represent everything listed in the terms list (Figure 2.8).

Figure 2.7

Sarah Pan

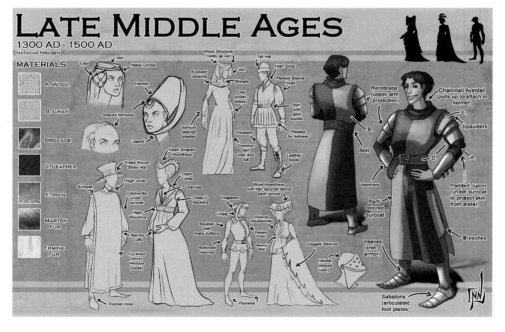

Figure 2.8

Natacha Nielsen

6. Always sign your work. The time you invest in your work has value and your signature supports that.
7. Consider your style guide as an information design all of its own. Once established, the layout can be reused over and over.
8. Consider your hierarchy and how you guide the viewer throughout the layout. A good design contains elements that lead the reader through each element in order of its significance. The type and images should be expressed starting from most important to the least important.

In layout design such as style sheets, I like to think of composition as a constellation – the brightest star being the first one you find in the night sky and the supporting stars that make up the whole of the constellation. That constellation may be one of a cluster of many constellations, so then we consider the push and pull, or the force of energy directional mass exudes, guiding all the aspects that make up the universe of your design.

These are some style sheets created for the Art of Costume class. In looking at these style sheets, examine each one and see where the design of the guide is compelling and where the student has captured enough information for a team or client to take the guide and use it as a production tool on a large-scale project. They should be able to do this based on the visual layout of articles, materials, shapes, and lines of the time period (Figures 2.9 and 2.10).

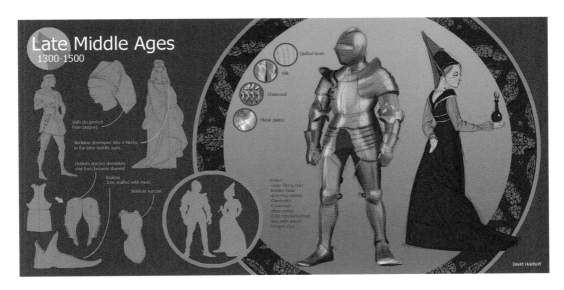

Figure 2.9

David Heidhoff

Figure 2.10

Amber Ansdell

Our goal in the weekly style sheet is to do a one-page document that would be part of a style bible or style guide for a game or production. In any style sheet, or style guide, there are key elements to consider in the design of the layout itself. The elements and principles to consider for layout design may differ from those for costume design, but some may overlap.

In the case of costume, some of the things you will want to consider are line, contrast, color, form, size, shape, proportion, texture, and rhythm. We will explore these elements and principles in more detail in Chapter 6.

As we look at the essential components for the layout in regard to costume, you will want to be able to convey the base style of the period and the patterns and motifs that support that style (Figure 2.11).

Consider having two more different viewing angles. The varying views are important factors to consider when conveying information to a modeler or someone planning on building your design in 3D (Figure 2.12).

Pay attention to the way in which you arrange your information. Establishing a hierarchy on each sheet is important as you take the viewer through the visual information and callouts you have chosen. For this module, I would suggest you establish a grid system to your sheet designs and stay with that design throughout the module, rather than reinventing the wheel each time. Please be creative in your layouts and the arrangement of information.

Figure 2.11

Jino Rufino

Figure 2.12

Nicole Chang

1. Layout – two-dimensional (2D) arrangement of information (Figure 2.13)
2. Materials – textiles, metals, wood, or other substances used in the creation of the costume (Figure 2.14)

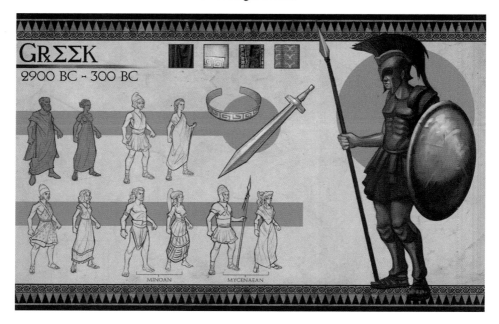

Figure 2.13

Omar Field Rahmam

Figure 2.14

Gilberto Arreola

3. Construction – how it is put together and taken on and off (Figure 2.15).
4. Solid hierarchy of focal points and supportive points – where the eye of the viewer goes first, second, and third (Figure 2.16)

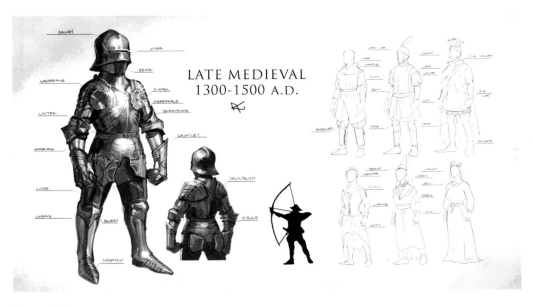

Figure 2.15

Ryan Savas

Figure 2.16

Amber Ansdell

5. Front and back views of the costume – or orthographic view of the costume (Figure 2.17)
6. Detail callouts and labels – labeling of costume components, accessories, materials, and information (Figure 2.18)

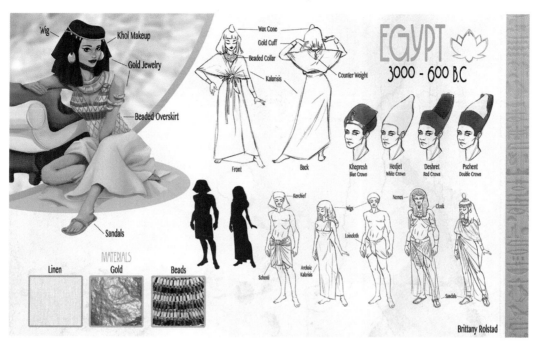

Figure 2.17
Brittany Rolstad

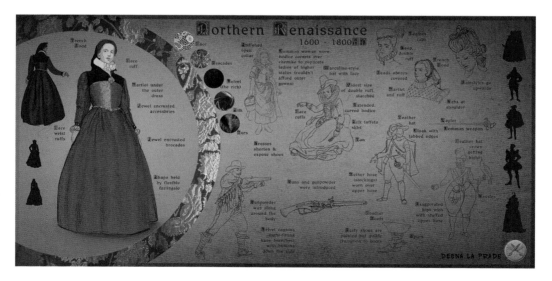

Figure 2.18
Deana LaPrada

7. Reference materials – from where the design springboarded (Figure 2.19)
8. Style language or motif for the period – patterns on fabric and style language for period (Figure 2.20)

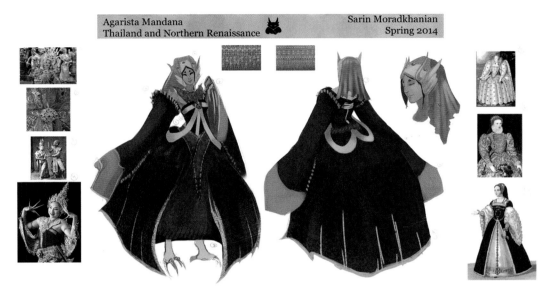

Figure 2.19

Sarin Moradkhanian

Figure 2.20

Brittney Rolsted

9. Color palette for each period – colors available for that time in history (Figure 2.21)
10. Accessories – bags, belts, jewelry, and anything additional to the costume (Figure 2.22)

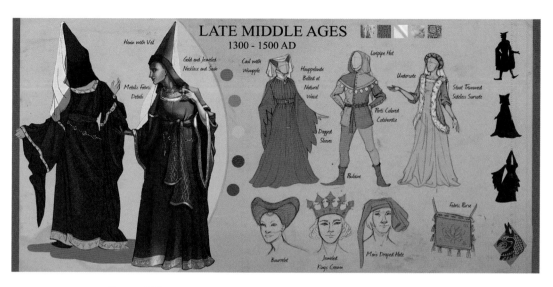

Figure 2.21

Talieson Jose

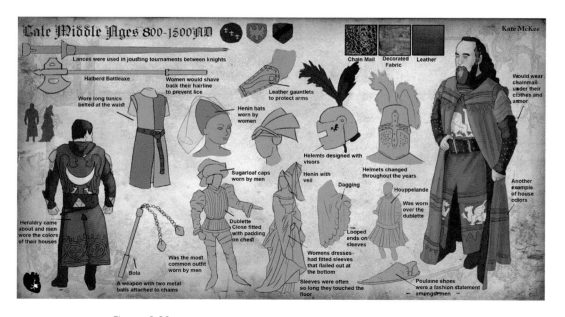

Figure 2.22

Kate McKee

2. Style Sheets

Remember always: *You are trying to captivate your viewer.*

Creating a grid system for the layout of large multifaceted projects is a valuable tool for consistency and time efficiency. You will want to establish the emphasis given to each aspect of the style sheet and then create a proportionate grid to utilize through all of the style sheet, design bible, or style guide that is the visual communication tool for the project. Leonardo da Vinci was one of the great designers who always considered the mathematical impact of proportions to his design. If you are not familiar with the golden rectangle, take a minute and look it up. This will give you a great starting point for establishing your focal point for the layout, which, in most cases, should be the featured costume. Jay Hambridge is another great contributor to visual layout design, along with Le Corbusier and his book, *Elements of Dynamic Symmetry.* The goal is to create a harmonic subdivision of space on your layout that will be utilized for all of your layouts to follow. It is much like reading a book with a consistent formula for the design of the information. Once the visual journey is established and repeated, you know exactly where to look for the callouts, title, materials, and all other elements required to communicate your idea. This speeds up the process for you and your viewer.

3

Thoughts on Character Design

Lou Police

Appeal. This is a word I've heard used many times in the Entertainment Industry as a general requirement for a successful character design.

The definition of the word "appeal", for our purposes, is the power to attract and grip the viewer's attention while creating some kind of emotional response. Whether it inspires or creates sympathy, fear, anger, humor, revulsion, etc., a successful character design must be appealing. If not, your audience becomes bored into apathy, wondering why they should care about or be interested in your character. The artist must also create a desire to get to know the character. Who is this person? What is he or she or it all about?

So, how does the artist visually create appeal in a character? In the initial design phase, there are only four ways: (1) facial expressions, (2) body type, (3) posing or gesture, and (4) costume

To successfully execute each of these four elements, the designer should have a thorough knowledge of human and animal anatomy, an experience with drawing the human figure both costumed and nude, the knowledge of the history of costume (past, present and future), and an experiential knowledge of basic drawing and design principles. In other words, the artist must be able to draw and design well.

So, with that in mind, what are some basic principles of good design as it pertains to creating a successful character for the Entertainment Industry?

There are many approaches we could take, but I have four thoughts that I think contain some of these critical, foundational principles.

First of all, let's consider a definition of design. My first design teacher in art school gave us a simple yet profound definition of what good design does.

He said that design means "one out of many". In other words, there are usually many elements or parts within a design, but they should all work together or flow together, visually, to create a unified whole. A good design has visual unity.

Another critical consideration revolves around the word "shape". What is so important about shape? EVERYTHING has a shape! Clouds, fire, water, smoke, fog, trees, rocks, a flock of birds, lions and tigers and bears (oh my!), human beings, an eye, a nostril, a hair style, etc. In fact, everywhere you look, shape rules! And don't forget that every project or production in the Entertainment Industry has a different shape language that the artist must adapt to and apply. The job of the artist, therefore, is to create visually interesting and intelligently designed shapes for people to feast their eyes upon. In other words, shapes that have APPEAL. We see through shape and the silhouette shape of any object the foundation of its design. It has also been said that "the silhouette is the building block of successful character design".

Words that come to mind when we consider the concept of "shape" are "streamlined" (sometimes the width of a pencil line can be the difference between a good shape and a great shape), "tapered" (parallel lines very often can be a design killer, while a tapered shape – thick to thin or thin to thick – is usually more aesthetically pleasing to the eye), and "geometry based". We see geometric shapes in nature, urban design, transportation design, architecture, product design, fashion, human and animal anatomy, and every other aspect of life.

Our third thought concerns the arrangement of the elements or parts within our overall design. They must be arranged in a thoughtful, intelligent, and aesthetically APPEALING way with structure and purpose, and that purpose is usually story driven. The story or narrative for which we are designing for should dictate all the aspects of the design process. In other words, our designs must constantly refer to and serve the story.

Much more could be said, but we will only touch on one last thought – the use of abstraction in the design process. Every great work of art has a beautiful, graphic, abstract design as its foundation or underneath its representational subject matter. It could be a silhouette or a dark and light pattern or simply some cool shapes.

Following these principles, and others, you should produce the appeal needed for the success of your character.

Design

Sandy Appleoff Lyons

Shape
Line
Texture
Proportion and Scale
Balance

Unity or Harmony
Rhythm
Emphasis or Focal Points
Movement
Process

Design is the heartbeat of your costumes and presents all the visual information you wish to convey. We are going to discuss some of the elements and principles of basic design as they apply to costume. In Chapter 2, we looked at design as it applies to layout and two-dimensional (2D) design; in this chapter, we will look at costume design (Figure 4.1).

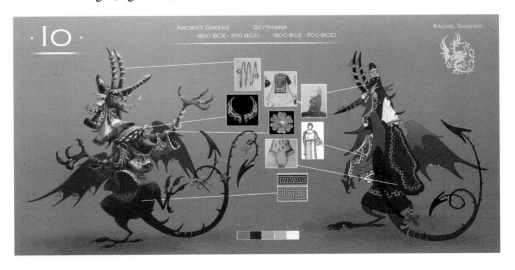

Figure 4.1

Rachel Skinner

The first class I ever taught was a fashion illustration class back in 1983. Barely out of college and sporting a passionate attitude for my newest endeavor, teaching, I used what I called the three "Cs" for my grading process. You will most likely run across this in other books on illustration and design because part of my syllabus has been published by several former students, as they applied it to their teaching careers. The three "Cs" are Concept, Composition, and Craft, and lastly I added Color.

In this book, we will look at Concept development, as the problem-solving process, leading to authentic, innovative costume designs. Composition involves all the elements and principles of design being applied to the costume itself – Craft being the level of execution of the design.

Since that point in time when the three "Cs" were my rubric, my criteria for my grading have grown. As time graced me with new markets and networks, my costume classes became targeted to the industry as it relates to games and films. It is applicable to the stage as well, but actually constructing a costume for stage or cosplay takes yet another level of construction knowledge of real elements, not virtual ones, and we will not address those factors in this book. However, one should note that the technology is now available for you to digitally create a costume and have it three-dimensional (3D) printed for construction.

In addition to information covered in Chapter 4, and moving into the costume itself, we will also look at "story" as it relates to costume.

Defining good design for innovative costumes has many variables. The basic elements and principles of design hold throughout any kind of design you are attempting, be it a structural, 2D, or 3D application. For the purpose of costume, design implements some basic elements and principles more than others.

The four elements first considered are shape and form, line, color/value, and texture. The five principles considered are proportion and scale, balance, unity (harmony), rhythm, and emphasis and movement, and lastly, the additional considerations are movement and pattern.

Shape

Shape language is the psychological response to various forms and is considered in relationship to the personality or guise; the wearer is trying to convey to the viewer? No matter what your audience, shape and form affect our subconscious and convey messages.

Examples are as follows:

Circular shapes: feminine, love, friendship, protection, compassion
Vertical shapes and lines: power, courage, dominant, masculine
Squares, rectangles, and triangles: power, stability, strength
Horizontal shapes and lines: peace, calm, quiet
Sharp angled shapes and lines: energy, anger, explosive, frenzy
Organic shapes and soft curves: happy, feminine, movement, pleasure
    (Figure 4.2)

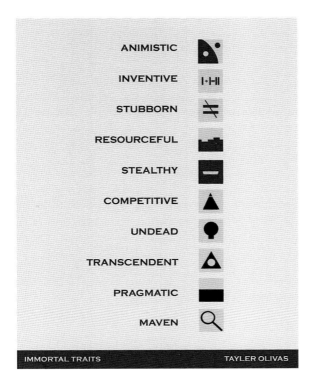

Figure 4.2

Tayler Olivas

Line

When we look at the line of a garment in costume, it is often in reference to the way the eye moves when looking at it or the overall impression of the garment. As an example, maybe because of strong verticals in the folds, detail, pattern or trim, and our eye follows that direction, which defines the line of the garment.

Line itself is an element of art defined by a point moving in space, and in costume it could be the way the eye travels in perception or the actual attributes of the costume itself. Lines can be straight, curved, full/shallow, vertical, horizontal, or diagonal, just to name a few. In rendering of the costume, they can be of any width or texture, and they can be continuous, implied, or broken to represent the details the creator hopes to convey.

Texture

In costume, texture means the way a surface feels or is perceived to feel. Texture can be added to attract or repel interest to an element. The shiny repetitive spots of metal buttons can draw the eye of the viewer up or down and get lost in the velvety mass of a full skirt. Texture is rough, smooth, metallic, velvety, gauzy, leathery, and finish offering different attributes of the costume (Figure 4.3).

Proportion and Scale

Using the relative size of elements against each other can attract attention to a focal point. A very large mass close to a small flat shape, the large mass will most likely be the first thing the eye is drawn to. When elements are designed larger than life, scale is being used to show drama (Figure 4.4).

Balance

Balance is defined as a state of equilibrium and equalized tension (Figure 4.5). It can be symmetrical or asymmetrical based on the division of space or shapes. It gives stability to your design. Many small shapes may balance one large shape. How you manage the balance of your design can create energy or calm. So if the design is not balanced, it is not an indication that your design is wrong, but it could relate to the personality of the wearer.

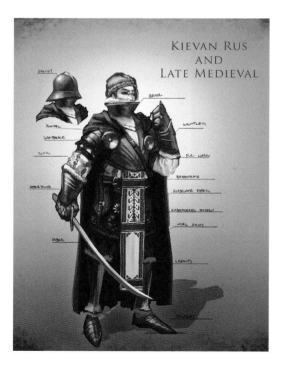

Figure 4.3

Ryan Savas

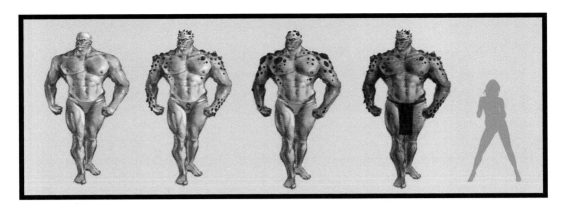

Figure 4.4

Bryant Koshu

Figure 4.5

Grace Kim

Unity or Harmony

This is a hard one to nail down because it works closely with balance, and you may not always want to use it. For the overall understanding of its use, it is the complementary combination of shapes, patterns, motifs, and details to balance the design as a whole. In color it could be any one of the many color schemes we are taught in color theory. When all elements are in agreement, a design is considered unified. No individual part is viewed as more important than the whole design. A good balance between unity and variety must be established to avoid a chaotic or a lifeless design.

If the designer is choosing to control the focus of the viewer, an overall unity may not be desired. As an example, perhaps some kind of dissonance is desired, and a clashing of color and shape is used to unsettle the viewer.

Rhythm

Rhythm happens when you use elements of your design repeatedly to create a feeling of movement. It creates mood. It is one of the strongest tools for guiding the eye of the viewer (Figure 4.6). You can find rhythm in the repetition of objects or details, and in the pattern of fabrics.

Emphasis or Focal Points

This is what catches your eye. Dominance is created by contrasting size, positioning, color, value range, style, or shape. The focal point should dominate the design with scale and contrast without sacrificing the unity of the whole (Figure 4.7).

Figure 4.6

Jino Rufino

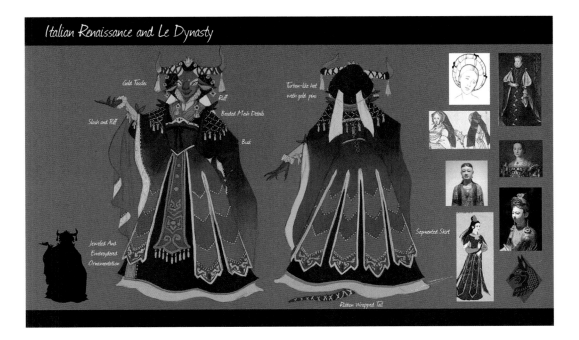

Figure 4.7

Talesin Jose

Movement

This can be the direction, rhythm, or speed that is perceived in looking at, or is actually performed by the costume itself. It may be the floating organza that is impacted by wind and gives flight to your design. It may be the path the eye takes in viewing, such as following a pattern in the costume that creates a frantic

Figure 4.8

Brittany Rolstad

feeling that one might see in the Jazz age or the strong vertical draped lines of the Roman toga (Figure 4.8).

Remember that each design is a composition. So the basic rules of composition apply. You want to guide the viewer on a journey. What are the star points in your constellation? How do they compare or create variety in your design? What is the design supposed to do, or how is it to serve the person wearing the design? What message should it convey? Here is where "story" comes into play. Consider all the aspects of your characters whether they are sloppy, neat, meticulous, adventure-some, shy, bold, or sly. Costume can motivate and alter perception. It can disguise or showcase. Many principles and elements that are true in layout design will hold true in design of the costume. However, in costume we have the universe as we know it or can imagine it, impacting the costume and the person in it. "Story" may serve as a tool as easily as a garment. That costumed character needs to be able to step out of the 2D world of the layout into the 3D world of games and films.

With the starting blocks created by using the breakout of historic periods, you can have a springboard that will help you get rolling faster. Once you have the rhythm down, you can start creating designs of your own.

Process

As you start your research, take special note of the motifs, patterns, shapes, influences, and functions of the clothing from the culture you have chosen. Usually the more contrast you have between the cultures studied in this book and the ones you research, the better it is. As you look at the pieces of the costume from your research, deconstruct it. Don't just take that really cool breastplate or pair of shoes from one culture and combine it with the garment pieces from another period study in the book. Tear it apart. Possibly look at the materials used beyond the fabrics. Those materials can be used in repetition to create something completely different. For instance, it could be a Polynesian culture that had shell necklaces and palm frond woven garments? A shell-beaded cloak with fronds creating epaulettes at the shoulders would be a fun deconstruct – reconstruct, for example, the early 1900s. So research, deconstruct, and then apply. You will find that every culture has differing shape languages and motifs that can be interwoven into your unique design.

Accessorizing designs is the icing on the cake. Those pretty little decorations serve a function. Of course, with cake, it is to entice the appetite, but with costume, accessories finalize the story. What does the character need to more clearly portray his/her function in the story? What does society dictate as proper for say, a lord or lady? Tell the viewer more about your character with the embellishments that kerchiefs, purses, pistols, swords, pocket combs, and tattoos can imply.

5

Immortals and the Creative Process

Sandy Appleoff Lyons

The Immortal Project

Josh Schelnutt

The Immortal project is a milestone test for you, the designer. Your first objective is to create your character, an Immortal that is not hindered by the constraints of time; no costume, no clothes, just the structural makeup of your character (Figure 5.1).

This project helps us use our ingenuity to create costumes within the boundaries of specifications or constraints. Why not just go for it, the sky is the limit? Actually, limitations help us as designers to deal with design problems in the real world, whether we are designing for imaginary realms or historically correct ones. They are not an obstacle; they are a challenge, and if you succeed, it will strengthen your skills as a designer (Figure 5.2).

Time is not an obstacle for your Immortals. He or she or it has watched cultures change, civilizations vanish, and possibly worlds evolve. How does their daily wear and dress wear change with time and travel? How do we create believable characters that captivate, make us laugh or cry, or move stealthily through the story from which they evolve, or dance through time with the world at their fingertips (Figure 5.3)?

We will journey deeper into character development, but first I would like to challenge you to create an Immortal to use as your learning tool as we travel through time doing tasks related to costume. Tasks such as going shopping, making, carving, and crafting the skins and clothing that disguise, or define the personality we develop.

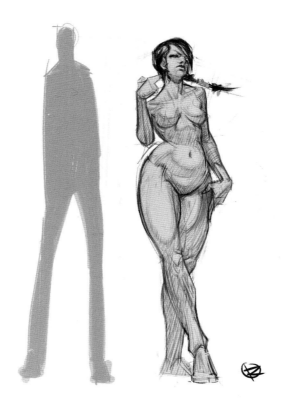

Figure 5.1

Robert Ortega

Figure 5.2

Veronica Liwski

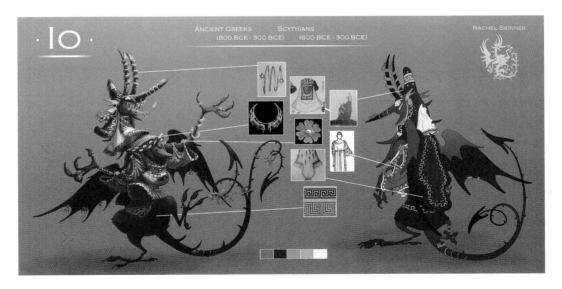

Figure 5.3

Rachel Skinner

The vehicle of story has throughout time been one of the strongest means of captivating the viewers and holding them, as the viewer explores your creation. Story can be told by the size of the pack on your back, to the holes in your shoes, from your shiny crown to the gauntlets on your arms. It is not just story alone, but all of the principles of design that play into strong design as well as story, so we are going to take the methodology of combining story, design, and cross-cultural, historically correct research to create our Immortals' costumes. Every two weeks we will select one of the cultures we have explored, and then combine it with a culture you will research on your own that correlates or is within the same time frame as the explored chapter in the book. The boundaries of sticking and building upon your story and the journey between two cultures and melding them together are a good mix for success. Some fabulous costume designs have come from this process and, throughout the book, I will be sharing the Immortals with you that my students have done (Figure 5.4).

Costume development based on period history is but one way to approach apparel design. Cultural history was, and is to this day, a direct impact on costume. The Immortal project was designed to use what was learned from weekly lectures, videos, and presentations about Western Civilization costume while you were a learner researching varying civilizations that were evolving around the world at the same period in time (Figure 5.5).

Figure 5.4

Samuel Youn

Figure 5.5

Bryant Koshu

In this course of study, I will continue to encourage you to draw from period-correct resource material and, if possible, design a period-authentic costumed model to build resource style sheets for each period covered in the book. I encourage you to keep limitations applied to your work. This will help you with learning specifics, honing your research skills, and increasing efficiency in time management.

How do we go about creating characters? Do go back and review Chapter 3 if you are having problems as we move forward.

I would like for you to make a list of at least ten personality traits or things that define the individuality of your Immortal. This may include where did he, she, or it originate, what do they eat, are they shy, do they like to laugh, are they clumsy, or do they have special powers? For each aspect, see if it can bring a shape to mind, then add that shape to your list behind the trait. We talked about this in Chapter 4. Happy may bring a circle to mind, and a mean attitude might bring a jagged lightning bolt line. Your list may look like this (Figure 5.6).

Whether or not these visual clues are used in the physique of your Immortals is not as important as it is thinking through them in respect to the costume you are going to design. Why did they pick something shiny as opposed to a cloak that hides their face? This is your story; the more thought that goes into your story, the stronger your design will be (Figure 5.7).

Figure 5.6

Eleanor Anderson

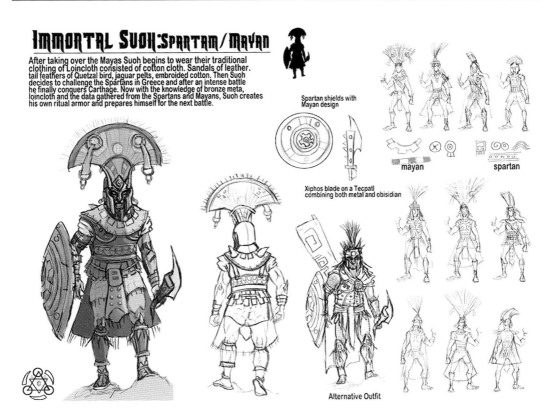

IMMORTAL SUOH: SPARTAN/MAYAN

After taking over the Mayas Suoh begins to wear their traditional clothing of Loincloth consisted of cotton cloth. Sandals of leather. tail feathers of Quetzal bird, jaguar pelts, embroided cotton. Then Suoh decides to challenge the Spartans in Greece and after an intense battle he finally conquers Carthage. Now with the knowledge of bronze meta, loincloth and the data gathered from the Spartans and Mayans, Suoh creates his own ritual armor and prepares himself for the next battle.

Spartan shields with Mayan design

Xiphos blade on a Tecpatl combining both metal and obisidian

mayan

spartan

Alternative Outfit

Figure 5.7

Gilberto Arreola

The Immortal Project

Create your Immortal and choose to stay with your creation throughout this learning process. Having one personality to build upon will help you focus on the costume design and the period history materials presented. My students in their first week of class are asked to lay out their style sheets of their Immortal giving as much information as possible about the person without the help of costume.

As we move through the weeks to come, consider every two to three periods covered the book and select a single time period to use. With that period, select a non-Western civilization that you researched beyond what is covered in the book corresponding to the time period. Again, this is about creating parameters for yourself. I encourage you to look at the ways that differing cultural artifacts can be combined to create innovative designs. Solid research will always be your best friend in stimulating the imagination and honing your creativity skills.

Good design in costume is going further than just combining pieces of existing clothing for that culture with another culture, but taking the structure, motif, accessories, and materials, and building something completely new from what you have learned. Deconstruct and reconstruct. Let's take a look at some of the successful Immortal projects coming from the class (Figures 5.8–5.13).

Figure 5.8

Jaime Stagg

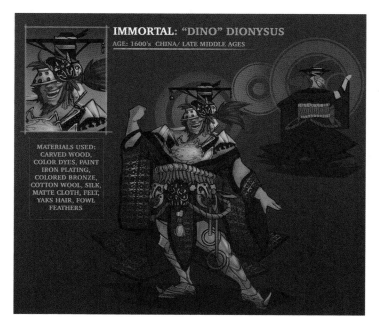

Figure 5.9

Amber Ansdell

Figure 5.10

Dylan Pock

Figure 5.11

James Bear

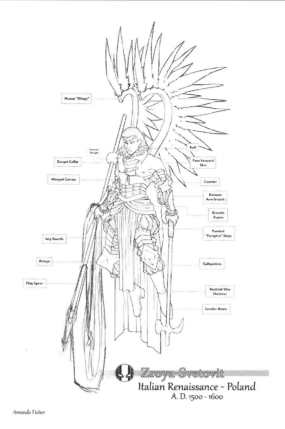

Figure 5.12

Amanda Fisher

Figure 5.13

Grace Kim

The design specifications or parameters are as follows:

1. Use the same Immortal throughout the journey through this learning module.
2. Use only two cultures in each Immortal design until you are through the book.
3. Pick only two cultures to use with the same historical time frame.
4. Do not just overlap or combine articles of clothing. Try to intertwine the garments, jewelry, motifs, and visual language from each culture to create something totally new. Deconstruct and then reconstruct.
5. Stick to your research.
6. Label the different parts of your costume.
7. Always do a front and back view being sensitive to the possibility that someone else may have to create a three-dimensional (3D) model or may build yet more characters based on your design. The more information you can provide, the better.
8. Utilize callouts for materials, specific points of connectivity, detail ornamentation, and historical reference.

If you do one Immortal sketch and then spend your time on the costume and not redrawing your Immortal each time, you will have better management of your time. There are instances when you will want to repose your Immortal possibly due to some climatic moment in the story or to accentuate some part of the costume. Good use of time is one more step towards success (Figure 5.14).

amber ansdell

Figure 5.14

Amber Ansdell

Throughout this book, you will want to look at color, shape, lighting, materials, focal points, and hierarchy of elements within the design as they relate to your costume (Figure 5.15).

Figure 5.15

Robert Ortega

6

Draping

Sandy Appleoff Lyons

Folds	Spiral
Pipe	Drop
Zigzag	Diaper
Half Lock	Inert

The clothed figure is much different to render than the nude one, but yet the landscape that clothing creates on the figure is dependent on the bedrock of the body underneath. Often a student sees the materials that clothe us in a different light if it is thought of in terms of landscape. The textiles and materials available today and throughout history give texture, pattern, depth, and definition to the body wearing them. Your journey is to systematically discover what differentiates the varying folds, based on weight of the material, direction of the weave, tensile strength, wear and tear, texture, and movement.

Let's first examine materials and then consider how they work with the body.

Weight of the material can vary from heavy leathers, sumptuous brocades, to beaded gowns, to the gossamer thin weaves of the finest silks. Our standard weights of silks, linens, and cottons fall somewhere in the middle. Each has a different characteristic when draped on the human or not so human form.

Linens which come from the plant fiber flax are much crisper in folds when ironed and starched or sized, and yet when warm moist conditions are introduced, the landscape of that fabric's fold it will completely change. This is but one small clue to telling a story with costume.

Brocades are one of the several shuttle-woven fabrics that came about in the Byzantine period and were first thought developed in China. Created on a draw loom, they are woven with both standard weft and supplemental weft. This twofold approach created an appearance to the fabric that embroidery could not replicate. The double weft technique provided a stiffness to the fabric design. Thus, it created a material sturdy and heavy enough for uses beyond costume, such as upholstery. When draped, it exuded a massive appearance to costumes making a landscape of rugged folds when crunched and voluptuous ones when draped.

Silk of insect origin is capable of being woven fine enough to carry a breeze and thus is seemingly the weakest of all materials, yet, in fact, its tensile strength is one of the strongest. China held its silk production as a highly revered secret. When the secret of silk worm production was revealed, the world embraced brocade fabrics through the centuries.

All fabrics, whether synthetic or natural, are impacted by thread count and weight of the thread or yarn itself. Fabric is weighed in GSM or grams per square meter, but we are not going to dive that deep into the technology of textiles when purchasing for construction. If you are building a costume, it may serve you to do a little investigating on your own. Textile history is a fascinating journey and one that will support your period-authentic designs based on place of origin.

Direction of the weave in relationship to the form will impact the folds of the fabric. When fabric is woven, the long strands connecting to the far ends of the loom are the warp. The second strand that goes back and forth weaving in and out of the warp threads is the weft. Pulling the fabric from warp edge to warp edge will not give much unless it has an elastic thread. However, all fabrics when pulled at a diagonal will give more. This is why the styles of women's dresses in the 1930s hung so nicely to their forms. That diagonal is called the "bias". The last term in regard to fabric layout is the selvage edge. The selvage edge does not fray, but the warp ends do.

Tensile strength, or the ability to resist breaking, of fabric changes with heat and moisture. The elasticity of the strands of many fabrics changes when either heat or moisture is in the environment or expelled from the body wearing them. Here again, another small visual detail in being able to tell a story with your costume.

This brings us to *wear* and tear. Depending on the character and how many dimes are there in his/her pocket, the abuse of the garment may be apparent. Elbows and knees are often worn out before other areas of an older garment. Hemlines can be abused by trudging through mucky byways. And stains and color change can appear from eating habits to fading from severe sunlight.

Texture is often determined by what is woven into the fabric, the coarseness of the strands, or how the fabric has been treated. Many of the early luxurious brocades were woven with gold and silver strands to not only create a beautiful reflective quality but also give them a sculpted quality. In the crinoline period, chintz fabrics were often painted with lacquers to give them a sculpted reflective quality without creating great weight. To this day we still starch shirts to make them crisp or find that we have to wash the sizing out of materials to get them to soften up.

Movement fabrics are often selected for garments based on the movement or activity they were designed for. As an example, tulle is used for ballet skirt or any other sheer skirt that is to stand out from the human form, and float if long and hold its shape if cut short as in tutu skirts. Its mesh-like weave allows exchange of air, letting it interact with the breezes around it, thus creating a floating sensation.

Folds

Now we move into the heart of the nature of the landscape and folds. George Brant Bridgeman was the first authored artist to define folds in such a way that every educator to follow has utilized his categorization to break down and understand the nature of folds.

I tell my students to think in triangles or diamond shapes when rendering folds, especially those with crisp fabric. Then soften out those shapes when dealing with softer materials.

All mass has directional force. Folds will define the mass, give volume to the figure, and help to bring life to the movement of your figure if mastered.

The fold structures we will look at are discussed in the sections that follow.

Pipe

Pipe folds can be multiple in succession, as you see on a curtain rod, or a shower curtain, but each creates a single semi-funnel shape for the fold. Or if you grab the fabric on the diagonal and pull, the stretch creates pipe folds because of the bias (Figure 6.1).

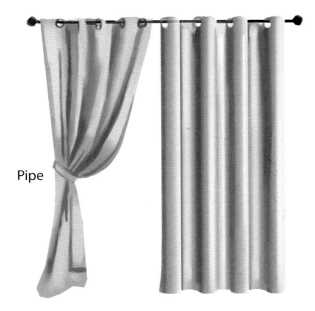

Pipe

Figure 6.1

Elenah Han

Zigzag

Zigzag is the alternating fold that happens when a tubular piece of fabric or material is bent, as you see at the elbow or knee. It alternates directions and visually appears in the diamond or triangular shape as discussed earlier (Figure 6.2).

Half Lock

When tubular fabric abruptly changes direction, you will get a half-lock fold. Understanding half locks will give strength to your costume rendering. Look at the way the fabric interacts with each directional movement of the arm. You will also get half-lock folds at the knees. Think about the fold form itself, and consider the change it will take as you move your viewing angle (Figure 6.3).

Figure 6.2

Sandy Appleoff Lyons

Figure 6.3

Tayler Olivas

Spiral

Again, often in tubular fabric forms, in the softer fabrics, you will get multiple wrapping folds following the contour of the arm or leg and following the direction of movement (Figure 6.4). In crisper fabrics, there will be more angularity. The spiral folds will help to define movement and shape. When a sleeve or pant leg is pushed up, you will also get condensed folds that are not complete spiral folds. Observe these folds for dynamics, depending on the action, these folds can appear diagonal.

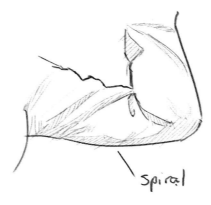

Figure 6.4

Vincent Vu

Drop

Here we see the diaper fold on the left and the drop fold on the right. A drop fold originates from a single point. Often in movement of this fold like on skirts, you get a wonderful flying fold as the leg moves forward. Masses of drop fold, such as you might see on a skirt of a gown, give the viewer the feeling of mass, which intensifies the visual dynamics (Figure 6.5).

Figure 6.5

Sarah Pan

Diaper

This fold is suspended from two points with the weight of the fabric determining the sag in the fabric in the middle. That sag may curve or be a crisp bend depending on your material (Figure 6.6).

Figure 6.6

Talisin Jose

Inert

It is possibly best drawn from your closet or bedroom. We find this fold at the bottom of very long gowns or in clothes discarded to the floor instead of a hanger. The fold angles originate from every direction. The mass is inert, but if there is an object below the mass, it will be defined by the movement in the folds (Figure 6.7).

Remember to vary the scale of your folds.

If you are drawing the draped figure with lines alone, try not to wrap those lines completely from edge to edge. If you have folds in a sleeve helping to define the shape of the arm under the fabric and the complexity of the fabric itself, keep some amount of space between the form edges and the edges of the fold. You lose visual strength in the fold if you do not. Try and draw your primary fold lines first, and then go back and indicate plane changes.

As you render clothing on the figure, look for your clues. If you look at a pant leg with the knee bent, you will have a drop fold from the knee and folds radiating from the bend point. The folds will compress in the area where the leg joins

Figure 6.7

Sarah Pan

the hips. Do not forget to consider what happens to the pant leg as it comes in contact with the foot. Next consider a skirt on a seated figure. Again, you will have drop folds from the knees and a diaper fold in the fabric between the knees, if the legs are not crossed.

I would encourage you to also look at the book *Dynamic Wrinkles and Drapery* by Burne Hogarth. You will find a different vernacular for the definition of the folds.

Folds, draping, and wrinkles are all visual clues for our audience to understand the story of the costume. Without them our costume has no personality.

7

Research

Sandy Appleoff Lyons and Jennifer Martinez Wormser

Books	Subscription Databases
Films	Websites
Periodical Publications	Ask an Expert

Research is imperative to developing good design methodologies. It helps to create a conceptual framework for any given project. Solid reference and citing of supportive materials expedite the production pipeline to create better time management across a team. First, for the visual information at their fingertips, and second, for the ability to dig deeper into a source for more information.

In the case of costume, fashion, and textile design, research helps us to better understand the historical impact of culture on clothing of a given period. It also gives us a foundational understanding of how technologies have been, and still are, feeding the palette of the capable designer.

Establish your research goal and define your problem.

1. Define your topic, such as historical costume by time and place.
2. Define the nature or mission of your research, such as clothing choices and/or designs that could potentially be made or tailored (your immortal's personality and taste).
3. Define the issues, such as technological development of textiles of the time or history of the dye trade and color choices.
4. Now analyze the relationships of everything you are exploring.

The more ideas and research you have, the more you have to draw from. If you are ending up with too many ideas, then begin to narrow down your ideation phase with things like motivation, personal habits of the character, physique, or moods.

Collect Reflect Plan Act.

Connect that which is not connected.

The objective is to inform our designs. Research can inspire, but it never replaces creative thinking.

For referencing and citing styles, you can look at the Modern Language Association (MLA) handbook, the Oxford handbook, APA, and Harvard AGPS.

The following is a contribution by Laguna College of Art and Design (LCAD) librarian and friend, Jennifer Martinez Wormser:

> The research tools and methods used by game art students to create costumes and accessories for their Immortals characters are a little different than what a "typical" undergraduate student uses for a research project. Because the assignment requires the students to use reliable, historically accurate references to inform their creative designs, the research required to successfully complete the project draws from a variety of sources and formats.

Books

Published books on both historical and current fashion and costume serve as strong research tools for the students, as many provide not only large, high-quality color photographs but also detailed information regarding the textiles and materials used. Historical survey books such as *Fashion: The Definitive History of Costume and Style* (DK Publishing, 2012) and the Kyoto Costume Institute's *Fashion: A History from the 18th to the 20th Century* (Taschen, 2015) offer students an opportunity to examine a range of international styles from different time periods. Other types of books that contribute to the research experience also include concept art publications and "art of" books for feature films, television, and games, which reproduce artists' drawings and ideation work, demonstrating what was proposed and finally selected for the end product. Viewing pages from these books can help students see the distinctions between a successful design and the multiple versions created as part of the process. Artist James Gurney, probably best known for his *Dinotopia* series, wrote a book titled *Imaginative Realism* in 2009, which best captured the goal of our students: to create something fantastic and imagined yet present it in a way that makes it authentic, realistic, and believable. Students who achieve these goals with their Immortal characters seamlessly weave historical eras from different parts of the world together to create a believable and realistic figure that heretofore did not exist.

Films

As visual learners, students in the game art program use and refer to films frequently as research for their own work, as well as for personal enrichment and entertainment. Feature films set in the future, the past, or in imagined worlds provide reference images for environments, vehicles, tools, and, of course, clothing and costumes for characters. A student may use the 2008 HBO series titled *John Adams* as a reference source for colonial-era clothing in the United States and also view the *Lord of the Rings* trilogy films by Peter Jackson for inspiration in designing the bodies, clothing, and weapons of fantastical and otherworldly creatures such as dwarves, orcs, goblins, and trolls. Tutorial films, whether offered through streaming services or via DVD, serve a different function and teach their viewers the mechanics to create, draw, texture, or paint. Some artists create their own tutorial films and sell them as DVDs or as digital downloads, and there are some businesses, such as The Gnomon Workshop and Lynda.com, that offer tutorial films via streaming services to teach the technical aspects of using software to create clothing textures, among other skills.

Periodical Publications

Periodical publications can serve as useful tools in researching fashion trends and histories; the Vogue Archive and Women's Wear Daily Archive, for example, are both offered electronically through ProQuest and provide a rich visual history of Western women's fashion over the past century. Earlier publications such as *Harper's Bazaar, Godey's Lady's Book,* and *Ladies' American Magazine,* the most popular women's magazine of the 19th century, featured hand-colored engraved fashion plates that were studied, copied and cut out, and framed. Many larger academic libraries may hold print runs or microfilm reels of women's magazines, and while a few more prominent titles such as *Vogue* are available electronically, these sources can be particularly useful for students wishing to use primary sources to research fashion and colors from a specific era.

Subscription Databases

Through libraries, students have access to subscription databases such as ARTstor, Bloomsbury Fashion Central, and Material Connexion to connect to other research resources related to historical fashion, the fashion industry, and material types. ARTstor allows its researchers to limit searches to the "fashion, costume, and jewelry" classification and draws heavily from the costume collections of various museums, featuring corsets, wedding dresses, headdresses, bracelets, bowler hats, and swords with detailed metadata and the ability to zoom in closely to study details in texture and stitching. We encourage students to use ARTstor in particular because of the detailed descriptive information that accompanies each image; students are able to pinpoint the historical and geographic features of the work accurately, lending an authenticity to the work they, in turn, create as a result of their research.

Websites

The websites of museums and research institutes related to fashion and clothing also provide students with useful and well-researched images of historic costume. The Kyoto Costume Institute in Kyoto, Japan, has a website that not only provides information about its exhibition, research, and publication programs but also has a portion of its digital archives available online. The Victoria and Albert Museum in London, England, has a robust website featuring online collections including embroidery, shoes, fashion, wedding dresses, and tapestries. The Metropolitan Museum of Art's Heilbrunn Timeline of Art History features concise curatorial essays – many of which also have lists of publications for further reading – such as *Fashion in European Armor, 1500–1600, American Ingenuity: Sportswear, 1930s–1970s,* and *Renaissance Velvet Textiles.* Emphasizing the reliability and authenticity of the website source is critical for students, who may find themselves tangled in their generic Google searches and find images that are inaccurately described or misrepresented from unreliable or unidentifiable sources.

Ask an Expert

Another resource we point students to is, of course, the research expert on campus – the librarian. Trained to evaluate resources and armed with an electronic rolodex of fellow librarian colleagues, students who work with the librarian to identify sources find their research process is often more efficient in terms of time and results. Through class presentations and other outreach activities on campus, librarians often express their eagerness to work with students and help them through the research process; the librarian may know of the unique materials in special collections or a new database subscription that can greatly enhance a student's collection of source material.

8

Translation into 3D

Sandy Appleoff Lyons, Jaime Stagg, and Anna Sakoi

In Chapter 1, Gavin Rich talks about the pipeline for games. Without getting too technical, let's look at what a concept artist needs to consider for the 3D artist to convert their ideas and designs to be modeled in 3D, and then moved into the game engine.

Sometimes there will be standards for concept layouts that companies will use. This may have to do with the poly count restrictions, or the scale and size that are needed to load the image into the program to expedite the modeling process, which then goes on into the game engine. Every asset or character has a poly count restriction. That is the total number of polygons it takes to draw your model in 3D space. There is no room for wasted polys here; every item must be considered.

This is why silhouettes are so important. The more information you can give the viewer by shape alone, the probability of it being a good source for an in game model, goes up.

Also the consideration of the details that can be painted into the texture map of the model, rather than using up polys on every detail, helps with keeping poly counts under control. As an example, a belt or buttons will be painted onto the torso model of the figure rather than being independently modeled out. Additional maps are then used to enhance the detail, light reflection, and opacity. Quickly summarized, each model can have three or more layers of additional maps that wrap the model emulating the look you are hoping to achieve.

The artist needs to be aware of the systems of measurement or layout guidelines when doing the final render of the sketch. The system of measurement should not hinder your creativity or drive your design, but consideration of the production of end product should always be at the back of your mind. Quite often your sketch is brought directly into the 3D program. And many times we only see one side of the asset in the game.

In costume it is all about the look, the character and the story. Changing the user interface or skin for a game character almost always includes clothing and/or accessories.

Costume designers are now becoming an important part of the pipeline for either designing or consulting in games, films, and toy designs.

Contribution by Jaime Stagg is as follows:

A quick little background on my LCAD education: I began at LCAD as an Illustration major and took an elective sculpture class. This became the pivotal moment in my education because it spurred me to explore other paths. I quickly fell in love with sculpture and realizing LCAD offered a Game Art BFA with emphasis on 3d character, and knew I had to switch majors.

During my LCAD path I took Sandy's Art of Costume class and something clicked for me. Early on in the class I was sketching and painting in the live model sessions, and honestly I struggled a bit with it. I eventually convinced Sandy to let me sculpt all the live model sessions and the immortal projects in Zbrush. This was so instrumental in my sculpting progression. I learned to sketch (in a sense) in Zbrush and speed sculpt. It created a bit of a monster out of me; from then on I just wanted all my art projects to be digital sculpting. I learned to sculpt different textiles and materials, from sculpting the heavy fabric weight of the brocade dresses in the Late Middle Ages to the structured under garments of the Baroque and Rococo. Unlike an illustration a sculpted figure is viewed from all angles, and by working this way throughout the class, it made me more curious about how exactly that cloak attached around the neck or how the ruffles on a crinoline were sewn underneath. Personally, I believe by sculpting you think deeper about the layers that make up the costume as a whole. Early on, I don't know how successful I was with my new-found passion but I stuck with it and I believe it created a yearning to continue; I knew I wanted my future career to involve sculpting clothing/costumes.

I am currently a freelance 3d designer working for Hasbro, making all kinds of toys, playsets, creatures and dolls from My Little Pony Equestria Girls to Star Wars Forces of Destiny dolls. (Are we allowed to name drop?) Many of the dolls I help create have sculpted clothing and accessories, lots of shoes, bags, belts, jewelry. For the Forces of Destiny line in particular, the dolls had a lot of sculpted clothing along with soft goods, ie cloaks or vests. Think of them like an action figure crossed with a fashion doll. Of course, I am only responsible for the sculpted parts, but there is a lot of overlap with all the clothes I had studied in Art of Costume, to what I am doing now, sculpting clothes for toys. During Art of Costume I didn't realize I had built an extensive mental library of how garments are constructed, how different textiles fall and how they look when draped over a body, which has been extremely helpful when I have been assigned a project with a lot of sculpted clothing.

Learning and sculpting garment construction in college has been very helpful to my career of designing costumes for toys. Many of the toys I now work on have moving parts and points of articulation. When you think of how a shirt is constructed, there are seams down the sides and seams around the shoulder where the arm hole is attached. This creates a natural breakpoint for the shoulder articulation. And to go a bit further, for production of a toy, sometimes the model needs to be hollowed out and halved. I like to use the seam lines of the clothing to determine where I cut the model. Then when the model is printed and put together, you can disguise the manufacturing lines within the construction of the clothing.

Up to this point I have written a lot about clothing, but a really important aspect of costume, and also my favorite part, are all the accessories. Sculpting accessories for toys really pulls the look together and finishes the costume. Whether it be a leather belt bag for Padme or a jeweled crown for a Disney princess, I feel is the most fun and is so important for telling story through a character, but perhaps I am a bit biased because with dolls sculpting accessories adds the finishing touches to a costume, like frosting to a cupcake.

When beginning to sculpt a toy I always start with a 2d design, usually an orthographic view of how the model/toy should look (Figure 8.1).

A little hack I learned is to crop the views into squares with Photoshop and import the images into Zbrush as textures. Within Zbrush open a Plane3D tool, convert to Polymesh3D then under the Geometry tab and Divide ×5. Select one of the orthographic views you loaded in as a texture and make sure to have RGB turned on, under the Polypaint tab select Polypaint From Texture. For the rest of your views, duplicate your Plane3d and repeat these steps and align them to their respective axis. Once this is set up you can bring append your base model and line it up with your ortho images and begin sculpting! I like this method because it saves with your tool. Make sure to turn off Dynamic Perspective (Hot Key "P") when using this method. But if you just want a quick and dirty way is to line up your mesh with a sketch, use the transparency feature "See-through" in zbrush and align the ortho image behind the program. This isn't always the best

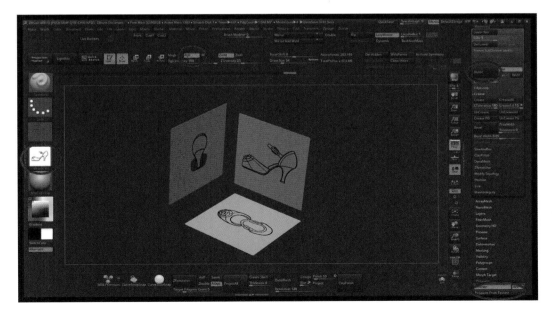

Figure 8.1

Jaime Stagg

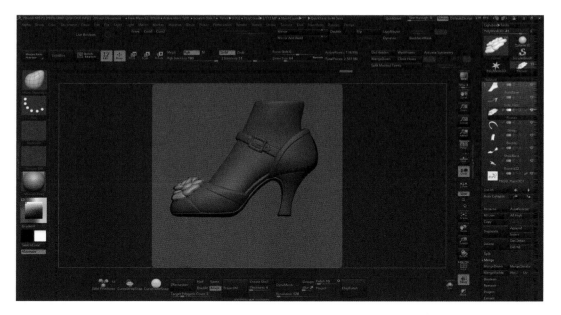

Figure 8.2

Jaime Stagg

if you are designing a more complex model that you need to work on over multiple days/weeks; but if you *are* using this method you can help yourself by saving orientations of your model, you can use Document>Zapplink and save views so you will be able to snap back to a specific orientation (front, back, left right, etc.). Once the image is aligned then I begin sculpting the body, it's so important to have a good foundation for the clothing to lay on even if it's going to be hidden under garb, especially when using Zbrush you can extract from the base model. It's the best way to create a base mesh for a shoe, or any other article of clothing (Figure 8.2).

I have a folder saved to my "Dropbox" of all the material samples, alphas and custom brushes I have made or collected since beginning Zbrush. I think it's so important to have these resources whether making toys or models for games. If I could give one more tip, it would just be to just practice sculpting as many things as possible!

For as long as I can remember, a hobby of mine has been making costumes, and I never thought my hobby could one day influence my career. I keep the same curiosity about how a garment is constructed to now figuring out how toys are made. When Sandy asked me to contribute to her book I was nervous but also honored. I am excited to have been able to reflect on how her class helped shape my career path. Keep sculpting =)

Contribution by Anna Sakoi is as follows:

Video games are a collaborative art form. A good team working together in sync can create something beautiful and inspiring. A costume designer/concept artist should work closely with all members of the team and have a strong understanding the entire pipeline in order to create designs that are appropriate for the product and easy to work with. As a 3D character artist at Super Evil Megacorp,

I work in close contact with our team's concept artists to create the heroes and skins for our game Vainglory.

Let's take a look at the job of a 3D character artist and how it relates to that of a concept artist. At my studio this job includes both modeling and texturing, but other studios might break up these disciplines into several different roles. Creating a 3D character entails interpreting the 2D design and turning it something that exists in three dimensional space. Depending on art style and personal preference a general workflow might look something like this: (1) a blockout to establish the proportions and shapes, (2) a high resolution model that has all the detail, (3) a low resolution to be used in the game engine, and (4) textures that give the model its surface properties such as color, specularity, et cetera.

As a modeler what I first want to see when I get a concept is that it has all the necessary information. This includes multiple views of the design. The most obvious and necessary views are front and back, but another extremely important view is whatever camera angle the character will be seen from in-game. For example, in the MOBA game the characters I work on are viewed from a top-down view and at a small size. Our game runs on mobile devices and on a phone screen our characters could appear half an inch tall. So it is good to design from that angle to plan for what the players will see. Some studios may also want you to do orthographic turnarounds. These are good in certain situations, but in my personal experience three-quarter views are more informative because you can get a better sense of volume and how elements wrap around the character. Also, it's hard to do accurate orthographic drawings where all the views match each other, and when they don't match, it may end up confusing the modeler more than helping.

The modeler also needs the concept to be brought to a satisfactory level of resolution, basically to the point where the modeler doesn't have to guess at what anything is. Loose and sketchy drawings and paintings can be very pretty, but they can also be confusing once someone needs to interpret them. Photo reference and material callouts are also very useful. For example, it's important to know what type of fabric something is because each one has very different physical properties and that will affect how it's sculpted and textured. It's very important for modelers to learn about costume in order to recreate concepts accurately.

When making clothing in 3D I usually try to create it with believable construction in mind. It's easy to fake something in 2D, but harder to do so in 3D when it's actually built around a body. Some modelers use cloth simulation programs such as Marvelous Designer. In that program the artist essentially makes a digital sewing pattern of cloth panels around a body, tells the program where to stitch them together, and then runs a simulation where the cloth is draped in a physically accurate manner. Since it's a simulation, the design must actually be functional for it to work.

Next, there are a few technical considerations to keep in mind. These factors are greatly affected by the platform the game is on. Vainglory runs on phones, tablets, and desktop computers. Phones and tablets have a lot less power than a PC or console, so the graphics are limited. The latest AAA games are much less restricted.

The first technical thing to think about is the triangle count. In essence, the game engine has to render the model piece-by-piece, and there's a limit to how much it can handle efficiently. Objects that are round, spikes, and cut out holes are some common things that use up a lot of triangles. This is because they need to affect the silhouette and therefore require geometry.

Another technical consideration is the shader and what textures feed into it. The basic shader for the game I work on uses only four texture maps: color, specular (grayscale), normal, and emissive. Each one controls something different about the look of the surface of the model. For example, specular and gloss maps determine how light is reflected and how glossy versus matte a material is. Vainglory's shader does not use a gloss map, instead it just has a constant value, and our specular map is grayscale, so it's impossible to create an accurate gold material since that would require a yellow specular color. It can be faked somewhat by adding a yellow color to the emissive map, but even so, distinguishing between gold and something like a clear coated acrylic paint material is not easy with our shader. This is a bit of an older type of shader and most shaders in use nowadays won't have this restriction, but it is an example of something to know about and keep in mind when designing. Proper planning will ensure that the design turns out as expected in game.

Another thing to know is the size of the texture maps. The textures in Vainglory are sized down to 512×512 pixels in game. That's literally the number of pixels that all the texture information has to fit into and it's not a lot. An intricate pattern may not be able to be represented well or clearly simply because there are not enough pixels. There are a few tricks that can help however. UVs are map of the model laid out in 2D and they determine where the textures are applied to the model. A smart UV layout, using symmetry and overlaps, can save space.

Speaking of UVs, something else I do sometimes is give more UV space to the more important areas of a model. Going back to what I said about the top-down camera angle for MOBAs, the most visible part of our game characters is the head and torso. So one technique to make the most of the space is to slightly scale up the head and torso UVs comparatively to the lower half of the body.

When making skins or alternate costumes for a character, there are a couple of special considerations. Skins can be a lot of fun - it's dressing up an existing character to be an alternate fantasy, but it's important to know how far it can depart from the original and how much it needs to stay the same. Typically a skin uses the same rig and animations as the original version of the character and the concept artist has to design within these restrictions. For example, you can't just add a long dress to a character who was wearing pants before. These types of designs can actually be quite challenging to make interesting because of these limitations.

In conclusion, this was just a brief look into the thought process of a 3D artist, but actually concept and modeling are just the first couple of steps out of the whole game art pipeline and there's so much more to learn about how rigging, animation, and visual effects work as well. It is all information well worth learning because in the end collaboration and understanding will lead to happier teammates, a smoother process, and more successful designs.

Egypt and Mesopotamia (3000–600 BC)

Sandy Appleoff Lyons

Egyptian Terms

It was hardly midday and already the sunlight was radiating off the sand along the river banks of the Nile. Chaney and Rae both walked with bundled sheaves of flax atop their heads having followed their father reaping in the fields. The flax harvest preceded the wheat harvest and was a necessary commodity for the creation of linen fabric.

> *The art of stiffening, pleating, and goffering (heating with irons to pleat) linen was practiced more lavishly in the later periods, than in the dress of the Old Kingdom. The color palette ranged from wine red, terracotta, yellow, green, indigo, and light blue, with much use of black and white.*

Flax was seen as the gift of the Nile and what few garments were worn were made of linen. Women's garments were often a single sheet of woven fabric wrapped in varying styles. Men and boys varied from loinclothes to shirt-like garments called schenti.

Their mother, an accomplished weaver, had just acquired one of the newer looms, making it possible to weave fabrics gossamer thin to heavier thicknesses. Chaney thought about her mother dressed in her kalasiris seated before the loom, where she wove her own fabrics, her nimble fingers moving the weft threads quickly through the warp threads strung on the loom.

> *The sheath dress was called the "calasiris", sometimes spelled with a "K". There were very few seams in costumes between 3000 and 300 BC. Tomb research is*

some of the best source for authentic clues to the costume of the time. Beaded sheath dresses withstood time and the paintings provided much of our information about the costume. Close fitting fabric dresses were also referred to as "sheath dresses" (Figure 9.1).

The width of the loom where the warp yarn was strung determined the width of the fabric, the yarn going across the warp was the weft, and the edges of the woven fabric were the salvage. The salvage edge keeps the fabric from unraveling or fraying. Salvage is the result of how the fabric is created. The edge at each side of the loom threads creates a salvage. Some of the finest weaves found were as high as 160 thread count in the lengthwise direction. The finest organdy fabric in the nineteenth and twentieth centuries seldom had 150.

Here is a simple loom example. A shuttle is a tool designed to neatly and compactly store or a holder that carries the thread across the loom weft yarn while weaving. Shuttles are thrown or passed back and forth through the shed between the yarn threads of the warp in order to weave in the weft. The simplest shuttles, known as "stick shuttles", are made from a flat, narrow piece of wood with notches on the ends to hold the weft yarn. More complicated shuttles incorporate bobbins and pins (Figures 9.2 and 9.3).

Figure 9.1

David Heidhoff

Figure 9.2

Sandy Appleoff Lyons

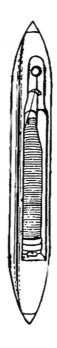

Figure 9.3

Sandy Appleoff Lyons

Chaney's reverie was interrupted as Rea took off at a dead run. His shaved head bobbing as his apron/loincloth billowed out, exaggerating his behind as he ran (Figure 9.4).

Figure 9.4

Ryan Savas

She then realized what had attracted him. He had ducked down behind the row of uncut flax, and she then revved up her pace to join him, feeling the earth between her toes as she ran.

Members of the royal family were actually walking their way, not being carried on sedan, followed by a long procession. The pharaoh wore the white hedjet crown.

CROWNS

- Blue crown (Khepresh)
  - Made of cloth or leather that was dyed blue
  - Used for coronations, victories, and royalty
- Red crown (Deshret)
  - Low ol of wadjet represented by snake/cobra head
- White crown (Hedjet)
  - Upper Egypt (south)
  - Symbol of Nekhbet represented by a vulture
- Double crown (Pschent)
  - Rulership of a united upper and lower Egypt (Figure 9.5)

His knee-length white schenti was covered by a second transparent schenti that floated as he walked, contrasted by the starched triangle of fabric hanging from his waist leading her eyes down to his woven curled toe shoes. Beside him, his wife walked in white kalasiris with her long dark hair crimped from pleating with the hot irons. Her arms were wrapped in gold cuffs, but neither wore the golden collars spoken of by her parents (Figure 9.6).

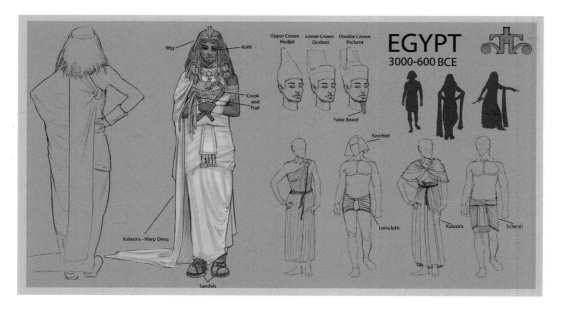

Figure 9.5

John Lam

EGYPT
3000 - 600 B.C.
NATACHA NIELSEN

MATERIALS

- GOLD
- LINEN
- SILK
- LAPIS LAZULI
- JASPER
- STEATITE
- WOOL
- QUARTZ
- CARNELIAN
- TURQUOISE

Necklace

White Crown of Upper Egypt

Red Crown of Lower Egypt

Combined Crown

Blue Crown of War

Hedjet · Deshret · Pshcent · Khepresh

Blue/white headdress

Decorative apron worn by upper class men/royalty

Gold collar also worn by men

False beard

Animal skin worn by royalty

Men shaved head under wig

Khepresh worn in New Kingdom

Women also wore lotus blossoms in their wig

Makeup also worn by men

Shent

Bracelets worn by noble men

Sheer overskirt began in Middle Kingdom

Scented wax cone

Locks of Horus or Youth (Royal boys)

Wig of wool or palm fiber

Khol eye makeup

Gold Collar with precious stones

Counter-weight for gold/gem collar

Flat topped crown with shaved head worn by Nefertiti

Some sandels curled at ends

Gold bracelets and jewelry inlaid with precious gems

Women wore earrings

Sheer Linen Calasiris

Sheath Dress or Calasiris

Flail

Crook

Linen dress wrapped about the body with minimal seams

Matching wrist and ankle bracelts

Rings of gold and precious stone

Kohl eye makeup

Beaded Calasiris

Nature inspired ring (Scarab)

New Kingdom - Shoes wore exclusively by people of status

Nefertiti was a symbol of beauty and fertility, often depicted in sheer fabrics

Sandels, worn by upper class

INN

Figure 9.6

Natacha Nielsen

Collars from bead work and metal work were worn by affluent and wealthy. Gold was prized by Egyptians. Silver, however, was not found in Egypt and had to be imported. Egypt was home to quite a few semiprecious stones, and they were used prolifically in costume and jewelry. Egyptian goldsmiths were very skilled.

The young boy between the royal couple wearing the lock of Horus, golden earrings, and a short schenti kept his gaze solemnly straight ahead in contrast to the somewhat joyful demeanor of the others (Figure 9.7).

The exotic dancers in the procession with dark kohl eye makeup around their eyes wore fabrics so sheer that it did little more than enhance their naked bodies (Figure 9.8)

Egyptians used cosmetics regardless of sex and social status for both aesthetic and therapeutic reasons. Oils and unguents were rubbed into the skin to protect it from the hot air. Most frequently used were white makeup; black makeup made with carbon, lead sulfide (galena), or manganese oxide (pyrolusite); and green makeup from malachite and other copper-based minerals. Red ochre was ground and mixed with water, and applied to the lips and cheeks, painted on with a brush. Henna was used to dye the fingernails yellow and orange.

They held their breath as the men in royal clothing, bearing the empty sedan chair on their shoulders, passed by followed by a line of men and women carrying flowers, and some wearing the cone of wax upon their heads (Figure 9.9).

For women the painted cones of wax came into play. New Kingdom women wore wrap skirts and sheath dresses, complex wrap dresses, bag tunics, shawls, long cloaks, sashes, and straps. Only people of status wore sandals on their feet if they wore shoes at all. Wigs were the standard. They were made of wool flax and palm fiber. Women's were longer than men's.

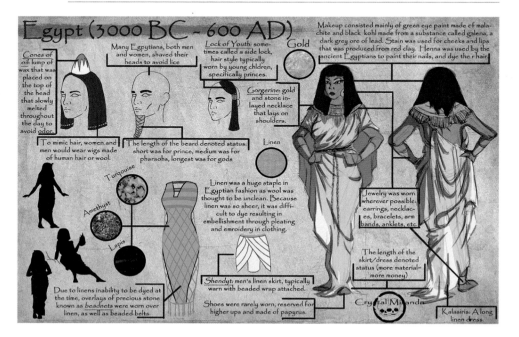

Figure 9.7

Miranda Crowell

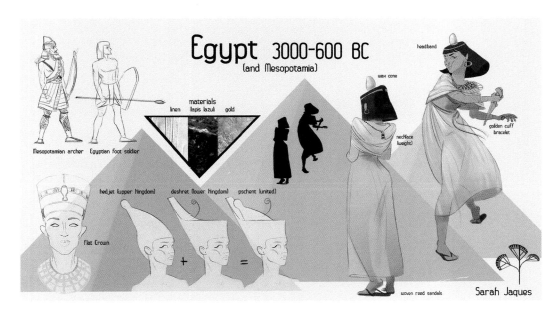

Figure 9.8

Sarah Jaques

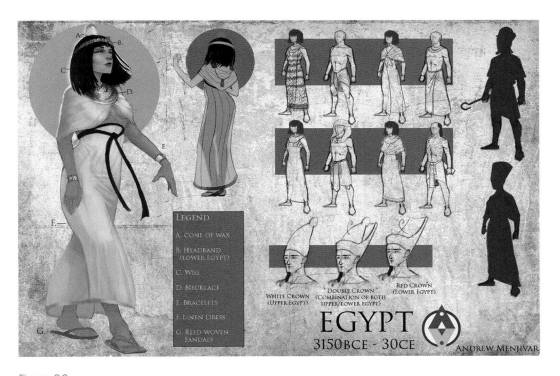

Figure 9.9

Andrew Menjivar

Both Chaney and Rae were often singled out from the other children, because they were quite young in appearance for their ages. Not 10 months apart they grew up like twins. Their parents had only to call one to find the other. Chaney thought of the stories from their grandmother about how others in their family were born with the mark, and that time would not touch them as it would their parents. The reality of the story was finally becoming a realization as they watched their parents age and time seemed to slow around the two of them. "You have the blonde spot on your heads", their grandmother used to say, "the immortal mark of royalty".

And Rae was off again, running like the wind as Chaney dismissed her reverie and followed in close pursuit.

EGYPTIAN TERMS

Drapery of cloth is more important than tailoring during this time period. Look how the Egyptians used intricate ways of folding cloth.

Sewing was used minimally because everything had to be hand-stitched.

MATERIALS

- Linen fabric – most common due to the extremely hot climate
  - Could be stiffened to create pleats
  - Made of flax
  - Generally kept white
  - Slightly transparent
- Leather and silk were received through trade and generally only worn by nobles
- Beads of semiprecious stone
- Loose ornamentation
- Gold
- Jewelry

MEN

Layer 1
- Loincloth
  - Worn mostly for protection
- Protection
  - Cloth loincloth was still worn underneath
  - Mainly used by soldiers and sailors

Layer 2
- Apron/loinskirt
  - Worn by common workers
  - Longer piece of fabric wrapped around the waist
  - Held up by either a sash or a belt
- Bag tunic
- Schenti (aka shendyt or kilt)
  - Held up by either a sash or a belt
  - Worn largely by nobles

WOMEN

Layer 1
- Loincloth (cloth)
  - Occasionally longer than men's similar to an underskirt

Layer 2
- Kalasiris (wrap dress)

  Archaic
  - Traditional (also worn by men)
  - Made out of a single piece of cloth
  - Draped over the shoulder

  Simple
  - Wrapped around the body (tubelike)
  - Could also be worn with either one or two shoulder straps for support

  Complex
  - Folds are more decorative
  - Sash was also worn with this
- V-neck dress
- Bag tunic

Layer 3 (optional)
- Overskirt
  - Beaded

OUTERWEAR (BOTH GENDERS)
- Shawls
- Cloak

HEADGEAR
- Caps
- Kerchief
  - Covers all or part of the hair
  - Could be worn short or long
- Wigs
  - Made of horse hair, flax, or palm fiber
  - Wax cones worn on top of them for fragrance
  - Worn by people who could afford it

ACCESSORIES/COSMETICS
- Kohl
  - Type of black eyes makeup worn by both men and women
- Collars
  - Wide intricate gold collars with beading and semi precious stones

SHOES
- Generally Egyptians went barefoot, unless it was a special occasion or rougher terrain

- Sandals
  - Made of either leather or papyrus

CHILDREN
- Most children would remain naked until around five years old.

PHARAOHS/NOBLES
- Animal skin/fur (other than leather) was something very sacred so only spiritual officials or pharaohs could wear them

NEMES
- Headdress worn by the pharaoh
- Made of cloth worn with the pharaoh's crown

False beads worn by female pharaoh to express strength associated with men. They were also worn my male nobility for ceremonial events.

- Power symbol

CROOK AND FLAIL
- Crook = kingship
- Flail = fertility (Figure 9.10)

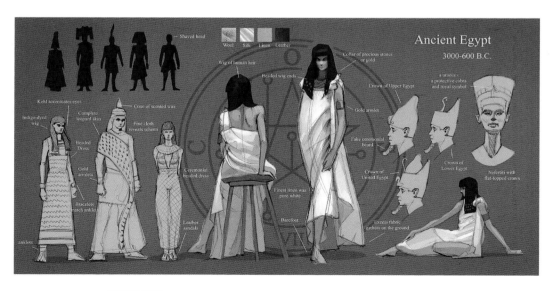

Figure 9.10

Andrew Tran

10

Minoan and Greek (2900–300 BC)

Sandy Appleoff Lyons

Linear A came much easier for Rae than for Chaney. Chaney contemplated the thought that she was better than Rae at the hieroglyphic and hieratic scripts that they had used in Egypt, but it was hard to keep up with him. She threw down her clay tablet, threw up her arms, and decided the day had much better things to conquer than another language. She dusted off her bell-shaped skirt that belted tightly to her tiny waist and headed in the direction of the palace Knonoss. The brightly patterned skirt moved fluidly as she walked and the hand-sewn fabric fitted closely to her body. The bodice took some getting used to. For her age she was fairly well endowed but even so, nothing like the older Minoan women. And to have her breasts exposed made her feel like a small child in Egypt again (Figure 10.1).

Like Chaney's skirt, many Minoan women wore skirts that flared out from the waist in a bell shape, with many decorations attached to the cloth. Ruffles or layers of gathered fabric were also quite popular. She tugged at her belt. They all had tiny waists though Chaney's natural waist was sometimes no match for the young women who wore the cinching metal belts since childhood. Now that she thought about it, she noticed that the boys and men wore the belts too.

A tiny waist was prized, and both men and women wore tight belts made of metal, which held their waists in. Some historians believe that these belts must have been worn since early childhood, forcing the waist to stop growing.

Many years had passed, but they still looked the same as they did in their teens. Rae, just like Chaney, had not aged. As she looked back over her shoulder, he stood

Figure 10.1

Paulina Carlton

much taller now, his back to her with the tassel of his skirt that covered his loin-cloth swinging like a tail. Many of the men had a decorative pagne pan-yuh or sheath or sheath that covered and protected the penis, and some had long aprons in the front and back with tassels or fringe. These small garments were made with much attention to detail. Loinclothes were made from a wide variety of materials, such as linen, leather, or wool, and decorated with bright colors and patterns.

While early Minoan men usually went bare-chested, in the later years, men often wore simple tunics and long robes (Figure 10.2).

Chaney loved to dance, and she twirled as she walked. That gift coupled with Rae's musical talent provided many a meal and shelter. However, her real fascination was with the colors and dyes used for woven threads and the painted patterns on many of the fabrics. She loved the saffron color derived from the spice trade and the purple dye extracted from murex mollusk, which produced a strong color-fast hue. It took a huge amount of these creatures to make a small amount of dye, and the Minoans incorporated much of the dye in their fabrics. Minoan women had an unprecedented love of color and display in their fabrics. Most designs were geometric, but the unprecedented love of nature themes produced many a garment illustrating flowers, fish, and birds in brilliant colors. The brightest of Chaney's wardrobe was a separated skirt brightly patterned in purple and saffron.

Minoans were one of the first to actually construct clothing that separated the legs. From the evolution of men's loinclothes to trunks, women in Minoan culture did the same with skirts creating what looked like an oversized guacho pant or cullott.

Figure 10.2

Jino Rufino

Figure 10.3

Sebastian Kings

Twirling around, she bumped face to breast with an older woman whose conical hat wrapped with a snake motif nearly fell off her head (Figure 10.3).

From all that Chaney could gather from their short time here was that this society was largely matriarchal. So she was not surprised when her apologetic look was met with one of stern consideration. Chaney's eyes then lit up at the sight of the beautiful gold work hanging from the woman's ears and wrists. The stern stare melted into a glow of shared appreciation for the accessories. Gold buttons beautifully chased and showing leaves and animal figures, and daintily wrought golden necklaces were layered like the rings on a tree. Technical skill is shown at its best in the necklets of granulated gold.

> *Bees have a symbolic and important connotation in many cultures worldwide. They were very important in the Minoan, matriarchal civilization. It is believed that the Great Mother of Mother Goddess was related to bees, while honey was used in rituals. As a symbol of the Mother Goddess, bees represent the mutual support and fertility (Figure 10.4).*

Figure 10.4

Sarah Pan

10. Minoan and Greek (2900–300 BC)

Chaney thought of Rae wielding his beautifully crafted double headed hand axe, and how beautiful the weapons carried by the men were. Though skilled with most any weapon thanks to the gift of time, Rae seldom carried one in this society. The look in his eyes were weapon enough as Chaney turned around to see Rae approaching. What had she done now?

Minoan

Custom tailored clothing to fit the figure. The Minoans had an obsession with tiny waists.

MEN

Layer 1
* Loincloth

Layer 2
* Tunic or skirt.
  - Skirts often had longer tail in the front or back.

Layer 3
* Long robe with belt

WOMEN

Layer 1
* Loincloth
  - Longer like an underskirt

Layer 2
* Bodice
  - Short sleeved
  - Occasionally with thin chemise underneath
  - Usually with breasts exposed (though it is disputed)
  - Bell-shaped skirt
  - Culott or gaucho type skirt

Layer 3
* Tight belt

SHOES

* Sandals

Conflict with the Mycenaeans, following the cataclysmic volcanic eruption, relocated the duo from devastated Crete to mainland Greece (Figure 10.5). Mycenaeans were a sophisticated and wealthy civilization and far more prone to warfare than the peaceful Minoans. It was most likely at this weak moment for the Minoans that the Mycenaeans choose to attack. Mycenaeans were known for their siege of the city of Troy, recorded by **Homer** in his two great epic poems, the "Iliad" and the "Odyssey". In the centuries to follow, the mainland would be home for Chaney and Rae (Figures 10.6 and 10.7).

Chaney and Rae – Greek

Greek history is customarily classified into three segments: the Archaic period, when peace prevailed from the north coast of Africa to the island and mainland Greece. The Classical period came next followed by the Hellenistic.

Rae looked at the horse with indifference; he did not share his sister's love of the creatures. Rae was barefoot, with his chiton thrown over his shoulder from the ride. Chaney was grateful that her brother indulged her with the things that brought her joy.

Figure 10.5

Adrian Romero

Figure 10.6

Andrew Menjivar

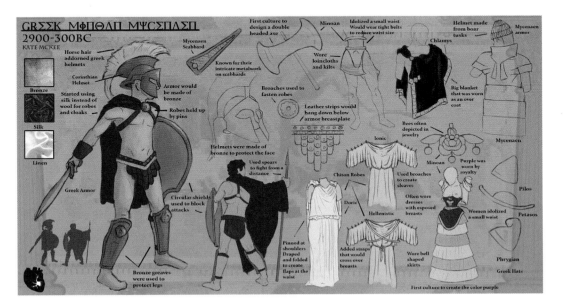

Figure 10.7

Kate McKee

In Greece, women were seldom graced with opportunities outside the home. They were usually weaving or keeping house.

The little secret journeys Rae arranged were the highlight of her days. It was quite a contrast from the Minoan society where women were held in such high regard.

Chaney, dressed in her chiton, thought the tunics and chitons of Greece offered a freedom of movement quite different in comparison with that of the Minoan fitted clothing. There was very little to no hand sewing in these garments. Being less fitted she found herself to be much more aware of the way she carried herself to convey the appeal she opted (Figure 10.8).

As the years passed they traveled from the tight, artificial lines of Minoan costume through the barbaric effects in Mycenaean clothing to the structured geometric garments of the Archaic Greeks, and eventually saw the whole process blossom into the beautifully draped, idealized yet natural clothing of the Classical Greeks (Figure 10.9).

Both Chaney and Rae wore chitons throughout their time in the Greek culture. The chiton itself changed with time. Rae's short Doric chiton was held at one shoulder with a fibula, while Chaney's was pinned at both shoulders. While both were belted or girdled at the waist, on the Doric chiton, the women's upper edges of the garment were folded over to hang down on the breast (Figure 10.10).

Figure 10.8

Breanna Guthrie

10. Minoan and Greek (2900–300 BC)

Figure 10.9

Grace Kim

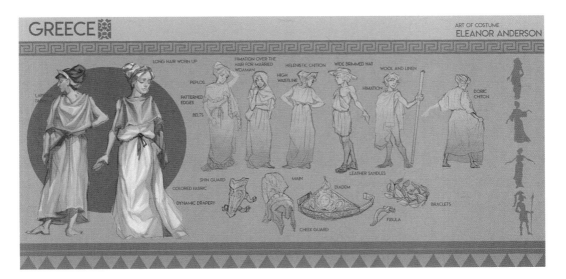

Figure 10.10

Eleanor Anderson

The women's Ionic chiton was cut with enough width from two pieces that were held together with fibula (pins). Going up the arm were multiple fibula or broaches holding the fabric into a sleeve of sorts. This garment was frequently pleated and long and sometimes trailing. It was often only sewn or caught together all the way down the right side with the left side left open.

Lastly was the Hellenistic chiton with the waistline or belting now going under the breasts. The Hellenistic Age was much wealthier and better shopped for fabrics as the conquests of Alexander the Great broadened the empire.

Yes, she could ride better than Rae and secretly had her own set of Spartan armor, but she did not have the ability to take another life. She wasn't sure that Rae did either. More often he was called out as a strategist. He did look majestic in full Spartan attire (Figure 10.11).

Chaney turned her horse, shaking her thoughtful reverie; she could feel eyes upon her. They were spotted, but too much distance for recognition. They heeled their horses and took off at full canter (Figures 10.12 and 10.13).

Figure 10.11

Sarah Jaques

10. Minoan and Greek (2900–300 BC)

Figure 10.12

Amber Ansdell

Figure 10.13

Natacha Nielsen

Mycenaean

- Although Mycenaeans adopted the style of the Minoans, women covered their breasts with a slightly transparent chemise underneath their girdle.

MEN

- Tunic
  - Short sleeved

WOMEN

- Long skirts occasionally tied with belt/girdle

Greek

MEN

- Perizoma – Greek for loincloth undergarment or for athletics
- Chitoniskos chiton – short between hip and thigh similar to the Doric chiton Archaic period
- Ionic chiton – short or long full, longer sleeves fastened with many fibula down from the shoulder
- Doric chiton – narrower without sleeves fastened with one broach at each shoulder
- Exomis – working-class short tunic pinned at one shoulder and cinched at the waist

WOMEN

Three basic chitons:

- Ionic chiton – held together with multiple pins going down the arm
- Doric chiton – broached at each shoulder with fibula
- Hellenistic chiton – empire waist line
- Fibula – pin
- Diplax was a small rectangular piece of fabric over the Ionic chiton
- Peplos – tunic made of one sheet folded over at the middle to look like multiple layers
- Himation was a large rectangular piece of fabric wrapped around the body worn by both men and women

11

Etruscan and Roman (800 BC–AD 400)

Sandy Appleoff Lyons

Etruscan and Roman

Chaney's large ceramic jar or amphorae was balanced nicely on her head while walking. The balancing act helped to increase her ability to focus her mind which often fleeted from subject to subject. Chaney felt less oppressed amidst the Etruscan people than in Greece and far freer now than she was in Rome. She thought of her clothing, remembering the brighter patterned chitons of the Minoan culture, she remembered herself in her Minoan chiton which had sleeves cut and sewn into the garment creating a slimmer fit. So much time had passed. The stola she wore today was simple in construction, not that different than the Grecian chitons, and it was girdled to make walking easier (Figure 11.1).

Remembering back to the island days, she could see Rae walking with his Minoan tebenna over his shoulder. Her thoughts then circled around to the devastation and the journey to Greece. While in Greece the chitons worn by both men and women were similar to Rae's Etruscan mantle he wore as they moved west. She could now see how Rae's mantle was the forerunner for today's Roman toga.

In Rome, their current home, everything was evolving.

The dress comparison between Greek and Roman women is quite similar. Both Ionic and Doric chitons were worn. The toga was an adaptation from the semicircular tebenna of the Estruscans and Minoans. At the age of 16 the plain white toga pura was worn. Understanding the toga folds and the poise to carry this elegant statement in simplicity took control and fortitude. The purest white toga candida was bleached and was worn by candidates for office. Toga Praetexta with a purple border was worn by young sons of nobility to

Figure 11.1

Brittany Rolsted

age 16 and young daughters of nobility until age 12. Toga Pulla was black for mourning the dead. Toga picta was purple with gold embroidery for generals at special occasions. Toga trabea was a multicolored striped toga assigned to religious officials that prophesized the future. Only male citizens were entitled to wear togas.

Note the first drape higher is the Umbo and the second drape lower is the sinus (Figure 11.2).

The Roman confederation changed everything. Julius Caesar's empire now spiraled across Europe and North Africa. Even with less oppression for women, only men were citizens and Chaney feels she has been defaulting to Rae for far too long now. She was working towards her own position and voice to be heard through this span of time.

The civilization of ancient Rome spanned more than a thousand years, with its beginnings of the walled city in the mid-8th century BC to the final collapse of the western Roman empire in 476 AD. In the beginning, the Romans derived much of their dress and lifestyle from the Greeks and the Etruscans. Once established the fingers of the Roman empire grew covering a vast territory – first that of the Etruscans, then the lands of the Mediterranean and Egypt. The great Roman empire escalated to new heights by the 2nd century and encompassed Spain up into the lands around the Black Sea, including Britain.

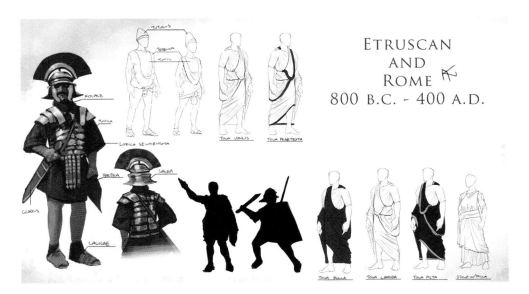

Figure 11.2

Ryan Savas

Figure 11.3

Sarah Pan

The sculpted dress of the Romans was a testimony to the architecture of the time. The Greeks were a strong influence, but the conquests engulfed many new cultural influences in the dyes and textile techniques that came into play (Figure 11.3).

Rae and Chaney now traveled extensively which was a relief. With the expansion of the empire, wider trading was possible. Chaney's knowledge and love of textiles and dyes were serving her cover for their timeless existence, since she now operated as textile merchant. She loved the cottons and silks from India and East Asia, how glorious were the colors and the weaves, all of which were embroidered with edging and fringing. Trading with China was also quite lucrative for them. But it seemed every ship they set foot on was monitored by the Roman legion. Hopefully soon they could afford their own ships and bypass the unwanted scrutiny. Chaney always had her eye on the dress of the people around her. She noticed that the Roman military had a hierarchy of clothing all of its own (Figure 11.4).

Officers wore an abolla, the draped rectangle of cloth fastening on the right shoulder. The sagum like the abolla was red. Soldiers wore it, but in times of war ordinary citizens wore it too (Figure 11.5).

Roman Terms

- Loincloth socks (udones)
- Leg wrappings and leg bindings (puttees)
- Trousers (Braccae)
- Military tunic (Tunica)
  - short- or long-sleeved
- Military belt (cingulum militare)

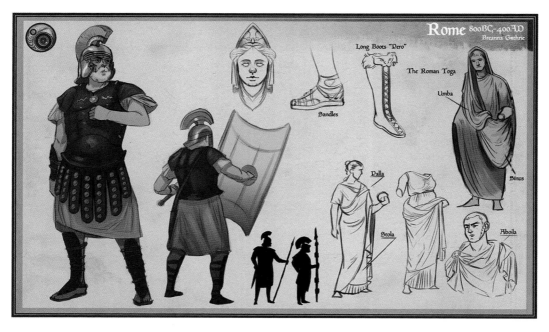

Figure 11.4

Breanna Guthrie

Figure 11.5

Jino Rufino

- Leather lappets
  - Apron/skirt of decorated strips (Pteruges)
- Armor
  - Corselet called the Lorica segmentata
  - Leather strap crossing the chest for free moment (Baldric)
  - Helmet (Galea)
  - Segmented arm protector (Manica)
  - Cloak (Sagum)
  - Hooded cloak (Paenula or Paludamentum)
  - Scarf (Focale)
  - Military sandals or boots (Caligae)

Rae opted to occupy the station of trader, wearing his tunic and solea. To keep his gift of conversation in the game, he stayed well acquainted with the current politics fueling the Roman campaigns. It seemed the fingers of Rome stretched everywhere into the world. His hair was long again, but he, as always, was clean shaven. Rae was not a slave to fashion, but he stood out in a crowd. His stature and carriage coupled with his congenial personality opened almost every door they needed opened. Usually it took wearing a toga to get attention from anyone in Rome, but on the open sea it was not practical. The togas were an art form all of their own. The carriage, the drape, and the fabric all made a visual impact and defined the person wearing it. With those broad shoulders Rae was stately when he needed to make a presence.

By nature, Chaney was a bit shy though she was quick to hide it. When need be, she would find herself pretending to be one of performers she had watched in the colosseum to create a wrap of courage around her when needed. Currently her only wrap was her palla. Chaney's hair was braided and pulled back, and she lifted the jar from her head and straightened her stola and brushed back the strands of hair from her face. She thought of the Roman matrons and their piles of curls and braids that were built up in architectural feats or pulled back under scarves or wrapped in vitta (Figure 11.6). Their station in life was often prescribed in their hair arrangement or the required veil or scarf. She never quite understood why they continually bleached their hair. Women of this part of the world had such beautiful dark curly hair (Figure 11.7).

As she reached the front door of their domus, a little beetle skittered across her sandal.

Women wore a stola, a palla, and a scarf or veil. They also bound their breasts under shear fabrics; this was called the brassiere or strophium. This garment was common among athletes and circus performers (Figure 11.8).

Figure 11.6

Alex Chung

11. Etruscan and Roman (800 BC–AD 400)

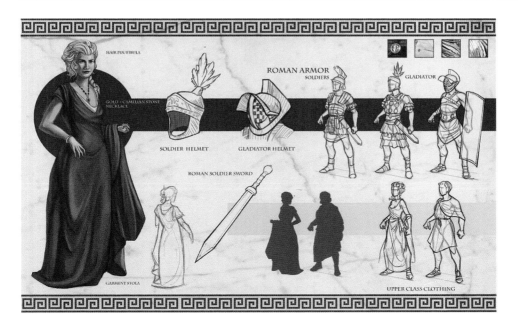

Figure 11.7

Omar Field-Rahman

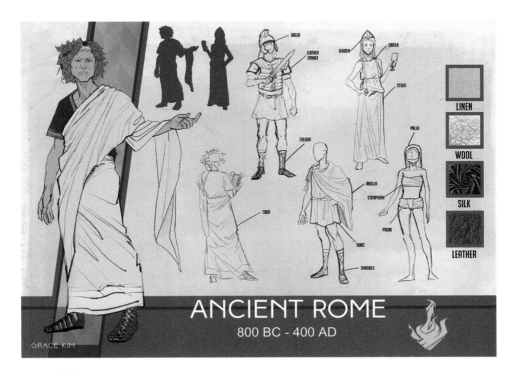

Figure 11.8

Grace Kim

Etruscan and Roman

Etruscan

MEN

Layer 1
- Perizoma loincloth

Layer 2
- Tunic

Layer 3
- Tebenna

Headdress – tutulus, a high-crowned, small brimmed hat

WOMEN

Layer 1
- Loincloth
- Longer like an underskirt

Layer 2
- Bodice
  - Pinned chiton, both Ionic and Doric
  - Occasionally with thin chemise underneath

Layer 3
- Tebenna

Headdress – tutulus

Shoes
- Sandals

Roman

MEN

- Tunic and toga
- Himation
- Boots – solea
- Pallium – cloak

WOMEN

- Stola fastened with fibulae
- Palla
- Mantle, similar to men's pallium
- Hair dress
- Vita, a woolen band to bind the hair (Figure 11.9)

Figure 11.9

Amber Ansdell

12

Byzantine/Early Medieval (AD 300–1300)

Sandy Appleoff Lyons

Early Middle Ages

The streets were raucous and filled with vendors, jugglers, holy men, beggars, and people of all sorts, even those selling everything, including themselves. The sun peeked through the colorful, roughly hung awnings as Chaney and Rae walked the streets. The vendors displayed exotic wares from the Orient and Middle East. There was not a mission to their outing today, besides maybe the hope of finding the vendor who, weeks ago, had the most aromatic and delicious spice selection. Their current home was not ostentatious, and smaller than in Rome; they have been keeping a modest profile since this was the longest they had stayed in one place. Time did not impact the young looking faces that now had centuries behind them, so moving was mandatory to avoid suspicion. How would a person that never ages be judged in the religious tones of the period? (Figure 12.1) The emperor Justinian maintained a tight rule over church and state, and his eyes were everywhere. The year was 546 and Constantinople was home.

During the years of Justinian's reign, the empire included most of the land surrounding the Mediterranean Sea, as Justinian's armies conquered part of the former Western Roman Empire, including North Africa. Under Justinian the domed Church of Holy Wisdom, or Hagia Sophia (532–37 AD) was built as were other great feats of architecture. Justinian changed the concept of state, establishing a Byzantine legal code that endured for centuries.

At the time of Justinian's death, the Byzantine Empire reigned supreme as the largest and most powerful state in Europe.

back view

mens wear

beaded hats

male and female sillouettes

womens wear

Figure 12.1

Amber Ansdell

Chaney was dressed in a white under-camicia and a long sideless stola or dalmatic of cotton decorated with lush designs from a jaccard loom. Her stola was belted, and the ensemble helped Chaney to blend into this colorful crowd. Her tunic had an open sleeve showing her white camicia. Women were modest but stately in dress. Very little skin was shown in Byzantium. And for that matter even Chaney's long braids were wrapped in a whimple (Figure 12.2).

Rae had on a simple hooded tunic with clavi going down over both shoulders and around the sleeve. His hose were not so modest, sporting a Persian pattern that was tasteful but a tad bit loud. Both Chaney and Ray wore short soft leather boots, calcei, that appeared humble in expense. It was the many years of wear to the very fine leather and lacking the jewels and color that kept their feet from being a focal point in their attire. Footwear was probably the most diverse aspect of clothing of the time. During this era, costume attained a richness of color, fabric, and ornament that far exceeded the greatest days of Rome. Elaborately designed jewelry was a hallmark of the Byzantine era. Pearls were plentiful and used lavishly with diamonds and other precious gems; eventually, colored glass beads and tiny mirrors were added to decorative embroideries (Figure 12.3).

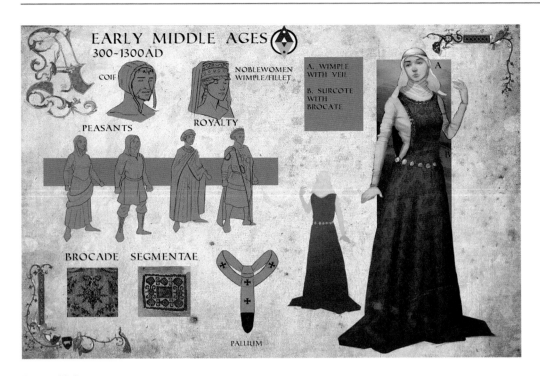

Figure 12.2

Andrew Menjivar

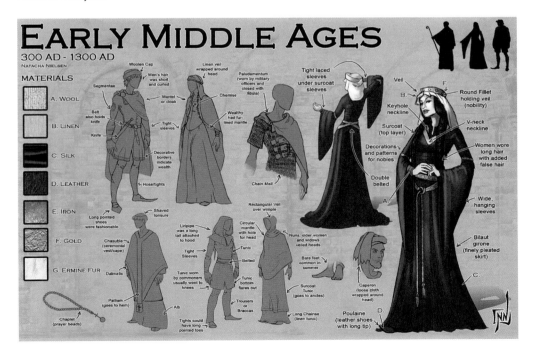

Figure 12.3

Natacha Nielsen

A uniquely Byzantine article worn at court was the tablion (sometimes called a claims), an ornamental jewel-encrusted, rectangular piece of fabric inset on men's and women's cloaks. The tablion identified the wearer as a member of the royal house or court dignitary. Another unusual garment was the Persian-derived maniakis, a separate collar of gold-embroidered, jewel-encrusted fabric (Figure 12.4).

The last stop today was the Hagia Sophia. The Hagia Sophia was awe inspiring. With its domed roof and beautiful mosaics just stepping inside the cathedral stopped Chaney in awe. The peacocks roaming the grounds were fun to feed. She began to see the colored clothing that denoted the differing stations at court as well as the clergy.

Religious garments seemed to make an impression on the attire of even the common people, as they adapted their style of dress that was founded in Roman influence. The clergy adapted attire from normal Byzantine garments like the dalmatica, and different components of the garments became representative of the varying aspect of the religious practice itself.

The Byzantine mode of dressing became more and more sumptuous until the fall of the empire. In addition, it provided the foundation for the liturgical costume of both the eastern and western Christian churches, particularly those of Russia. Garments originated by the Byzantines are still worn today by members of the Eastern Orthodox Church, and the influence of the Byzantines can be seen in the robes and headwear of leaders in the Roman Catholic Church (Figure 12.5).

There was no longer a law to govern the wear of garments so Chaney and Rae had the freedom to wear clothing that exposed their true wealth. The purple dyes cherished for so many centuries were stockpiled in Chaney's reserves. She seldom saw it worn among the merchants, traders, and locals, but for special occasions

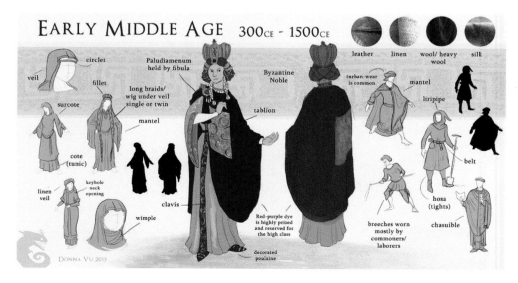

Figure 12.4

Donna Vu

Figure 12.5

Grace Kim

Figure 12.6

Samual Youn

the emperor and his wife were dressed head to toe in flowing silks of purples and jewel-encrusted detail. Most clothing was layered. Men sported tunic and trousers under their dalmatica and women layered under their stolas with camicia, and then finished with a paludamentum or long cloak (Figure 12.6).

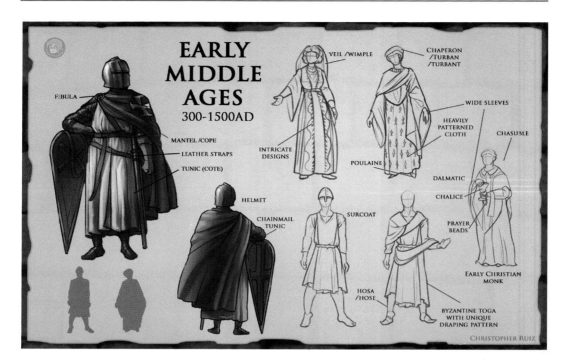

Figure 12.7

Christopher Ruiz

Chaney now had a small parade of peacocks following her, but her small bag of bread crumbs was now empty. Rae, waiting with never-ending patience, signaled her it was time to go (Figure 12.7).

Early Middle Ages Terms

MATERIALS

- Linen
- Leather
  - Fenestrated
- Wool
  - Warm + water repellent
- Ermine
  - Weasel fur for the wealthy
- Silk
  - Worn by wealthy
- Red dye
  - Very difficult to get, worn by royalty
- Necklines
  - Keyhole
  - V-neck
  - High collar

- Tunics are generally tight but flow out at the hips.
- Top layer tunic would contrast in color from the bottom layer

Clothing
- Breeches
  - Short pants worn by commoners
- Hosa/hose
  - Tights, worn by more wealthy people
  - Occasionally had leather soles
  - Worn as pants
- Trousers/braccas
  - Could be worn over tights
  - Mostly seen by commoner/soldiers
  - Worn during the hotter weather
- Tunic (cote)
  - Commoners wore them to the knees
  - These get longer as time goes on
  - Usually people wore two, the bottom contrasting to the top layer (surcoat)
  - Clavi – stripes + patterns that show rank/wealth
  - Segmentae = decorative medallions
  - Belted with knife
- Mantle
  - A cloak
  - Cope/cape
  - Wide cape with hood
  - Liripipe, a long tail attached to hood
- Paludamentum
  - Cloak worn over the shoulders by military officers
  - Closed with fibula
  - (Optional) Tablion, a piece of square/diamond cloth or leather with pattern

Headgear/Hair
- Chaperon/turban/turbant
  - Loose cloth wrapped around head
  - Woolen cap
  - Short and curled

Clothing
- Chemise
  - Thin garment worn underneath dress
- Tunica or dalmatica
  - Double layered (top layer referred to as surcoat)
  - Top layer sleeves longer
  - Clavi – stripes + patterns that show rank/wealth

- Segmentae = decorative medallions
- Ankle length
- Bliaut girone = a long blouselike garment worn by both men and women
- Mantle
  - Cloak
  - Furlined if rich

Headgear/Hair
- Veils/wimple
  - Worn over long hair
  - Occasionally worn with metal circlet
- Long hair
  - Braided in one long ponytail or twin tails

Shoes
- Poulaine
  - Leather shoes with long tip
- Calcei leather boots
  - Either heavy or tailored
  - Tailored, worn at the ankle

Religious Wear
- Chasuble
  - Ceremonial vest/cape worn by clergymen
- Sakkos
  - Fancy tunic
- Dalmatic
  - Long wide sleeved tunic
- Chaplet
  - Prayer beads
- Sclavien
  - Coarse tunic worn by pilgrims
- Palium

13

Late Middle Ages (AD 1300–1500)

Sandy Appleoff Lyons

Late Middle Ages

Quite some time has passed since Chaney and Rae moved across the Mediterranean. Rae was gainfully employed as paid protection; this was now the norm as the feudal system waned. Chaney actually was better with a bow than Rae, but his reaction time and speed still far surpassed hers. This was not a day and age for a woman to be part of warring factions, but if she could get away with it, she did. The dress for women was cumbersome, and she was continually hiding her close cropped hair with long braids of horsehair. Between famine and the plague there had been enough loss for both the siblings, so they chose their guise and battles wisely (Figure 13.1).

Taxes enable the rich to buy their armies rather than recruit for noble causes. Contracted armies were more dependable than the 40 days required to serve feudal system. Warfare had changed from horseback combatting to using longbow, and now the importing of gunpowder (Figure 13.2).

Sixty percent of the population were now gone due to the Black Plague.

Capitalism was on the rise, and with that, Medieval guilds grew. When not on horseback in the guise of a man, Chaney was active in the textile guilds bartering for textiles and dyes, feeding her passion for color and fabric (Figure 13.3).

Figure 13.1

Sebastian Kings

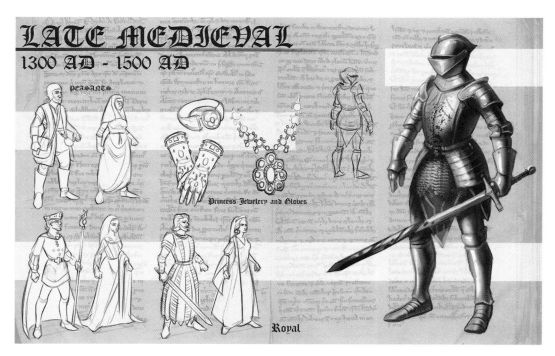

Figure 13.2

Omar Field Rahmam

Figure 13.3

Jino Rufino

The textile guilds and dye guilds were somewhat a secret society, protecting their formulas and taking care of their own. The importation of indigo for blue dye was banned by Charlemagne as he tried to control the trade by using European crops that produced the desired colors.

Today she sits in the market stall with skeins of yarn and rolls of fabric. Her disguised hair coifed on each side and pulled in up in cauls, with a lovely silk sample hanging draped between them.

Her new kirtle itched. Most likely the linen needed to be soaked one more time. Her Cote Hardie was modest and her surcote was a fine weave and not overly detailed so as not to call attention to her station. She was starting to see narrow sleeved dresses with rolled down collar V necks replacing the houppelande, and the waistline was starting to rise (Figure 13.4).

The sumptuary laws kept Chaney from accessorizing with gold or silver, but she had an excellent collection of buttons for sale. Now that they were actually functional and not just ornamentation, her creative spirit gave rise to replacing the glitter of precious metals with shells, ivory, and other materials. The royalty of the time was so over the top with ornamentation that Chaney thought it sad, considering the extreme economic gap between the upper and lower classes (Figures 13.5–13.7).

Figure 13.4

Paulina Carlton

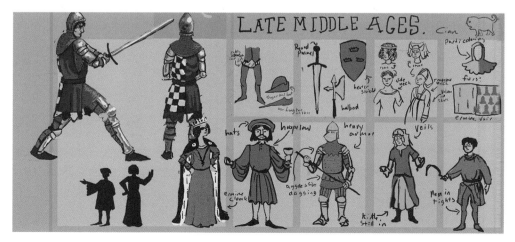

Figure 13.5

Max Gerber

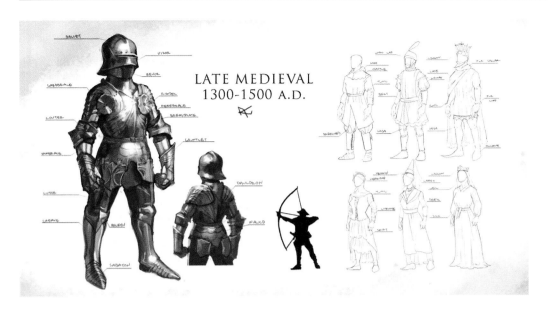

Figure 13.6

RyanSavas

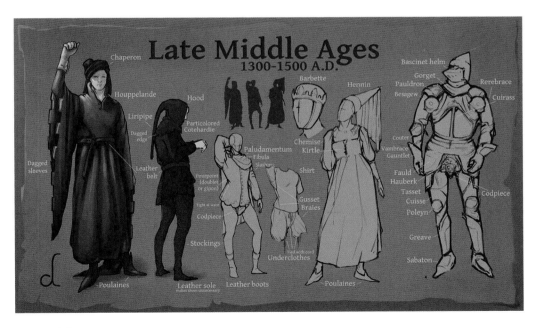

Figure 13.7

Dominic Camuglia

The sumptuary laws of the time regulated the dress for both men and women. Because Chaney sold many of the costly fabrics, she was allowed special considerations for her wear.

Rae having worked his way up through the ranks enjoyed much freedom in his choice of apparel. He was now often in his doublet rather than the pourpoint and possessed a fine coat of armor. Doublets were based off the pourpoint. There are sometimes as many as 22–25 pattern pieces to a doublet, and they were constructed to fit close. Doublets were made from silk and then linen for the battle field. Today he also wore a short houppeland leaving his surcoat at home. Indigo dye was now finding its way to Europe, and Rae's doublet was beautiful hue of blue. Dyes were expensive, but Chaney had connections.

The spinning wheel and the horizontal loom with foot treadles and shuttle simplified the production of textiles and clothing. Increased production encouraged increased consumption of textile products and clothing resulting in the beautiful costumes we associate with medieval Europe. Trade later improved with new territories due to the Crusades and Marco Polo. Attractive clothing became more available and affordable, and the emerging middle class began to emulate the styles of the elite.

Rae took exception today and joined Chaney in her stall. As she bartered and fussed with her display of wares, he crafted out little melodies on his recorder. The small flutelike instrument he often carried with him turned many a head toward the stall by the lure of tunes he crafted so well. He paused looking down as a chicken ran by trying to flee from the hungry hands pursuing it. He laughed and then considered his shoes, his poulaines, thinking the shoe did not nearly have a long enough tip, a mental note for tomorrow and a musical note for today (Figures 13.8 and 13.9).

Figure 13.8

Matthew Moony

NINA MODAFFARI

Figure 13.9

Nina Modaffari

Hats and headgears were all the rage in England and France, but in Italy the fashion was a bit softer and more natural. Chaney was stopped by the French accent of the woman at her stall. She was seeking the sheerest of silks for her hennin. She was familiar with the tall hats of the northern Europeans but wouldn't be caught dead in one herself. How could anyone get anything done spending their day balancing a flimsy pointed hat on her head? And to make things even harder, a weight of fabric at the point. She bit down on her lip to gather her smile into a controlled expression of sincere interest.

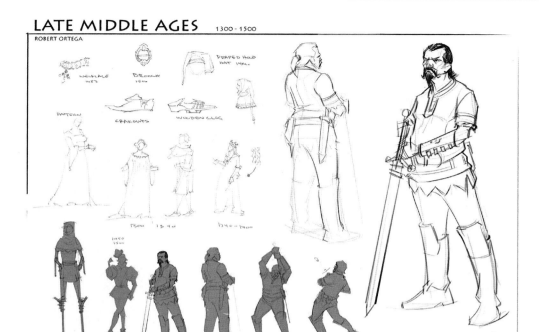

Figure 13.10

Robert Ortega

Purchase complete and coin in hand, Rae helped Chaney to drop the wooden front to her stall. The look between them was one of understanding, time for a pint (Figures 13.10 and 13.11).

Late Middle Ages

MATERIALS

- Linen – weight depends on the wearer's status
- Leather – fenestrated
- Wool – warm + water repellent
- Ermine – weasel fur for the wealthy
- Silk – worn by wealthy
- Red Dye – very difficult to get, worn by royalty
- Necklines – going from rounded and square to much lower V-neck lines
- Silhouette – going from fitted bodice to high waistlines for women
- Many colors into play and decorative elements like dagging
- Parti colored
- Heraldry

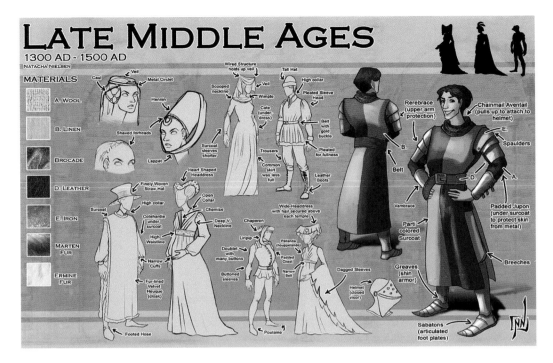

Figure 13.11

Natasha Nielsen

CLOTHING

- Cote and surcote early on both men and women

MEN

- Pourpoints – holding up stocking with ties from four points inside the cote
- Doublets – worn with hose varied in length and grew shorter as time went on.
- Houppelande – replaced the Cote and varied in length
- Large distinctive shoulders come into vogue in 1450
- Breeches – short pants worn by commoners
- Hosa/hose
    - Tights, worn by more wealthy people
    - Occasionally had leather soles
    - Worn as pants
- Trousers/braccas
    - Could be worn over tights
    - Mostly seen by commoner/soldiers
    - Worn during the hotter weather

- Tunic (cote)
  - Commoners wore them to the knees
  - These get longer as time goes on
  - Usually people wore two, the bottom contrasting to the top layer
- Mantle
  - A cloak
- Doublets, sort upper body garments worn with hose. They grew shorter with time
- Cotehardie
  - Cope/cape

WOMEN

- Close fitting bodice and skirt for peasant (sumptuary laws)
- Close fitting tunic or kirtle
- Surcote
- Cotehardie
- Houppelande
- Flattening bust corset
- Ruffs and small collars
- Fullness lots of fabric and trains

Headgear/Hair
- Grew in importance

  Women
  - Whipple loose cloth wrapped around head
  - Hennin
  - Caul
  - Bourrelet

  Men
  - Woolen cap
  - Chaperon/turban/turban
  - Sugarloaf caps

Shoes
- Poulaine

14

Italian Renaissance (1400–1600)

Sandy Appleoff Lyons

Italian Renaissance

Chaney was immersed in the textile guilds and, over the years, earned a reputation that was hard to conceal. During the years as she moved from one part of the Italian peninsula to the other, Chaney eventually claimed to be her own daughter, while amassing a small fortune in holdings with her corner on the velvet market. The families that controlled the trade secrets had been part of her life for almost a century now. Italian velvets and brocades were the most highly valued products of the talented silk weavers of Italy and were exported all over Europe, as well as to the Ottoman Empire (Figure 14.1).

Italian velvets were first developed in Lucca in Tuscany. Due to invasions and political upheaval, many exited to Venice where the velvet guilds were independent of even the silk guilds. Florence soon became competitive in the 14th century on through the 16th–17th centuries. Velvet weaving is an interesting process. If you would like to know more, I would recommend reading "Renaissance Velvets" by Lisa Monnas.

Storefronts of the fabric vendors were proliferous and the siblings owned several throughout Italy, but passing shoppers particularly paused at those owned by Chaney and Rae to admire their wares. Laws actually regulated dress at this time, and the working class was not afforded or allowed the luxury of dressing like the upper class, though they often tried to emulate them. It seemed that each year the "guardaroba" or the set of clothing that was made up of two layers of indoor clothing and a mantle was allowed more additions as time went on and clothing

Figure 14.1

Brittany Rolstad

construction changed. The guardaroba was a set of clothing made up of three garments: two layers of indoor clothing and a mantle. Sleeves, being detachable, could be changed to create differing looks, and the wealthy were allowed the additional layering of skirts that marked their status (Figure 14.2).

The natural form fitting bust line that laced up the front gave way to a stiffer and more structured, almost sculpted attire that had a bodice foundation of a "basquine", precursor to the corset. Chaney enjoyed modeling what could be accomplished with her luxurious textiles, but after a day of cinching up for the correct silhouette, she was glad to undo the lacings of the cinch and breathe more easily (Figure 14.3).

Her morning would start with first her "camicia", the "gamurra", and then her "giornea". She would tie on her sleeves and pull out the elegant red camicia between the ties or rolls of her sleeves at the shoulder. She had procured the carmine dye from a trader coming in from Spain and immediately set up a contract for more. For walking in the muddy streets Chaney occasionally chose to wear the "chopines", which were an art form all their own to walk in, but tried

Figure 14.2

Taliesin Jose

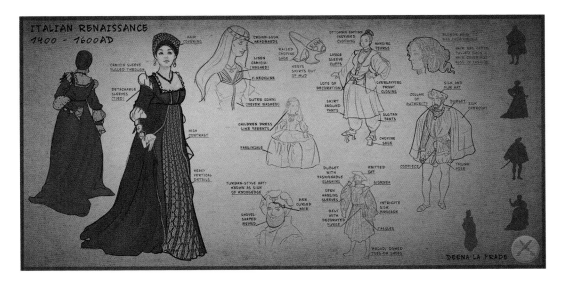

Figure 14.3

Deena LaPrada

her best to hide her leather boots, which were far more comfortable, under her skirts. She hired a Spanish boot maker to craft her a pair of boots with higher heels to deal with the mud, but they were not fashionable for a virtuous woman (Figure 14.4).

Chaney's blond hair was radiant under the *trinzale*, a fabric cap covering the back of the head. It was held in place by a thin jeweled string, a *lenza*, which lay across the forehead (Figure 14.5).

Rae was an astute business man himself choosing to handle the goldsmiths who provided the metallic threads for the rich brocades when he wasn't enjoying company with the musicians and the rebirth of the classical arts. Rebirth and reborn were words that fueled the word "renaissance".

He had the physique and the posture to do justice to a handsome doublet. His doublet had a short peplum, and the bodice had minimal slashing* showing the exquisite red silk of his camicia through the cuts. With this, he wore knee-length breeches and silk brocade hose. He had considered wearing his sleeveless jerkin today, but the weather was cooler than normal, and he was meeting new traders. The colorful tunics and red hats so often seen on those hobnobbing with the powerful families were slowly being seen less and less.

The Victoria and Albert Museum in London defines slashing as "a decorative technique that made regular, spaced cuts into the fabric of a garment, hat or shoe".

Figure 14.4

Gabrielle Navarro

Figure 14.5

Eleanor Anderson

I have read that the fashion or fad developed from the pillaging of a dead soldier's clothing on the battlefield. The damaged clothing was further enhanced with cuts and underclothing pulled through the cuts (Figure 14.6).

Figure 14.6

Breanna Guthrie

He had a small ruff collar on his camicia that he liked to consider as his contribution to fashion.

The trading Rae and Chaney did around the continent over the centuries placed them on the forefront of trends, bringing technology and ideas from as far east as Asia, and as far west as Spain and the Netherlands. They now owned two ships that operated under a subsidiary, captained by a man that interestingly enough, also seemed to defy time.

Today cargo was moving northward by horse and wagon, and on board were two passengers from the West. Their silhouettes varied from the Italian fitted doublet. Their doublets were padded in the front creating what he learned is called a "Peascod belly". It was belted lower and looked a bit goose breast shaped. The shoulder of their jackets were also padded, creating a strong square shape that exaggerated the shoulder width. Rae's eyes radiated humor as he stole a glance at their cod pieces, which were quite exposed from rather full breeches. The padding must be a needed sign of strength. The breeches, better known as trunk hose, had panes of fabric looping from the waist to the thigh where they were secured. Topping off their attire, the caps were almost crown-like and tipped to one side (Figure 14.7).

Rea pondered, thought that as the balance of power changed in the West, so would the look accepted by Italian men. He was already considering what his trade in metallic threads and accessories might bring to the future of fashion in European trade. The Baroque period was on the horizon and there was a fortune to be made (Figures 14.8–14.10).

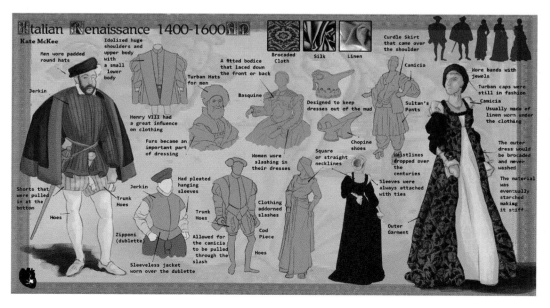

Figure 14.7

Kate McKee

14. Italian Renaissance (1400–1600)

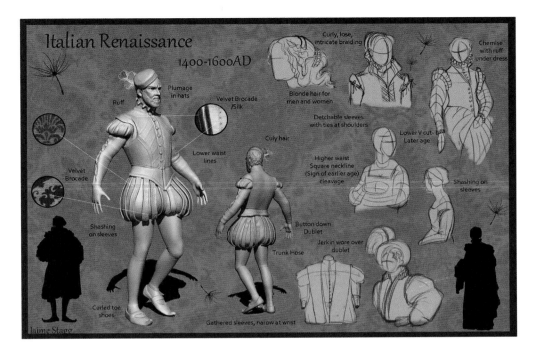

Figure 14.8

Jaime Stagg

Figure 14.9

Paulina Carlton

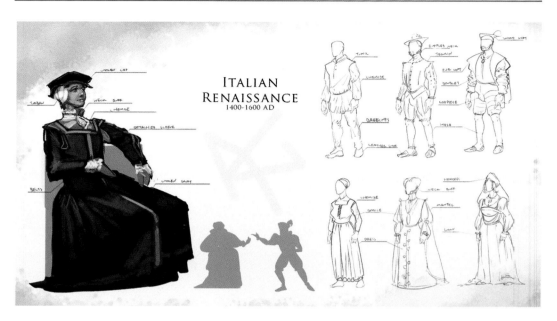

Figure 14.10

Ryan Savas

Italian Renaissance

MATERIALS
- Linen
- Leather
- Wool
  - Warm + water repellent
- Silk
  - Worn by wealthy
- Brocade
  - Rich decorative weaving; done with silks, gold, or silver
- Ostrich feathers
  - Worn on hats
- Velvet
  - Black is high class
- Fur
  - Necklines – square; high with ruff collar; low cut
  - Silhouette – buff top for men; tight ridged, with poofy slashed sleeves; large collars
- Colors
  - The Renaissance color palette featured the reds, realgar and carmine, and among the blues, azurite, ultramarine, and indigo. The greens were verdigris, green earth, and malachite; the yellows were Naples yellow, orpiment, and lead-tin yellow. Renaissance

browns were obtained from umber. Whites were lead white, gypsum, and lime white, and blacks were carbon black and bone black.

Clothing

- Hosa/hose
  - Tights, occasionally had leather soles
- Trunk hose
- Codpiece
  - Protective and decorative wear for the genitals.
- Camica/chemise
- Peascod belly
  - Popular for a time, padding underneath clothing, aka goosebelly
- Doublet
  - Male fitted bodice
- Jerkin
  - Usually sleeveless jacket
- Zipone
  - Belted tunic worn over the knee

Headgear/Hair

- Turban
  - Chaperone of wrapped cloth

Clothing

- Camica/chemise
  - Thin white undergarment made of linen; loose
- Ruff
- Giornea outer tunic
- Kirtle is still worn by lower class; tighter skirt occasionally has straps.
- Basquine, derived from the medieval cottes and surcotes, consisted of a tight fitting, sleeveless bodice worn over a shirt and laced at the back.
- Gamurra (dress) of Florence – also known as the camora and zupa; this was the basic term for "gown" from the 1300s to the 1500s and was worn by all classes in a variety of colors and fabrics. This unlined dress could be worn alone, with or without matching sleeves. Starting in the 1540s
- Gown/dress
  - Bodice (upper ridged part) or basquine, top part stiff, would have tight sleeves
- Mantle
- Cloak
- Furlined if rich

Headgear/Hair

- Crowns + headbands
- Turban

Shoes

- Rounded tops
- Chopine
  - Worn by women; tall shoes, go over shoes – clogs

Northern Renaissance (AD 1500–1600)

Sandy Appleoff Lyons

Northern Renaissance

The air iced her breath as she stepped into the cold. Political and economic power was shifting westward, and it was Rae's decision that they follow it. Chaney shivered; she really didn't mind the cold, but her clothing kept getting more and more cumbersome. She pulled up her skirts as she stepped onto the snow-covered street facing the canals. The noise of the hoists from the cargo ships was muted by the new snowfall (Figure 15.1).

Figure 15.1

Taliesin Jose

The chemise was still the undergarment for women. Gowns were then placed over the chemise with a fitted bodice. Skirts were long and full, flaring from the waist to the floor, often trailing into trains in the back. Women either wore a single dress or two layers consisting of an outer skirt which might be divided or looped up in front to display the contrasting skirt of the underdress like you see here on the left. Trains on outer gowns were often buttoned or pinned back at the waist to show the train lining. So we are potentially looking at three layers for outer garments. We still have square necklines and V necks which evolved into high necklines with wing collars. Sleeves included smooth fitting narrow, wide funnel shapes with contrasting linings and hanging sleeves (Figure 15.2).

With the French invasion of Italy, France had interfered with Italian affairs, which led to many of the Italian ideas, styles, and artists moving westward. This was thought to be the end of the Italian Renaissance. Chaney and Rae chose to head even further northwest. It was Spain's Golden Age and it had become a wealthy power. The Netherlands regions were territories under Spain's rule, and Chaney and Rae's current home. Home was now a prosperous trading port, and a hub for lace trading, which was driving the fashion statement of the time. Chaney's desire for lace made it timely for the move and also a good business

Figure 15.2

Gabrielle Navarro

venture coupled with her textile empire in Italy. The drapers guild, a business agent for textiles in the Netherlands, and a largely male-dominated group controlled much of the textile trade. Their neighbor down the street was commissioned to do a painting of the syndics, who warden the textile/drapers guild. His name is Rembrandt.

Rapid development of needle and bobbin lace started in earnest in the early 16th century in the Venice and Milan areas of current Italy and in the Flanders (which is primarily Belgium today, but also a part of what is today Holland) in Northern Europe. The very fine linen threads from Flanders, imported silk threads from China as well as gold and silver threads were used to make the fine laces. Cotton was not used for making lace until approximately 1830 (Figure 15.3).

Chaney and Rae were both involved in moving marketable products for lace production back into their Italian production. Chaney worked largely with the linen thread producers from Flanders and Rae with the silver and gold threads coming in from the Orient. Both went into the production of the stiff lace used for the wisks and falling collars which were becoming all the rage. The Dutch also favored the oversized ruffs which brought giggles to Chaney whenever she saw

Figure 15.3

Brittany Rolstad

the circular formation of looped fabric larger than the person's head ringing the neck of the wearer (Figure 15.4).

Like an ode to repetition of the circular shapes ringing the neck, many ladies adopted the French farthingale, that was the structural undergarment for defining the shape of the skirt.

The repetition in form definitely made a statement. But Chaney preferred the conservative choice of the somewhat natural cone shape of her skirts, which made for practicality when sitting and crossing thresholds (Figure 15.5).

> *The first changes in silhouette came in the first quarter of the century with the change of Spanish farthingale which was more cone shaped, with a bum roll, in comparison to the French farthingale which was like a drum.*

Spanish influence increased the size of ruffs to new grandeur. They became so large that they had to be supported by frames called the "supportasse". We will see this again in the future in the Medici Queens of France. Wisks, too, took on new shapes and proportions (Figure 15.6).

Chaney pulled her hood up over her coif and conch and headed toward the docks. The shipments should be unloaded by now, and she hoped to catch Rae before the inspection of the cargo.

Figure 15.4

Paulina Carlton

Figure 15.5

Samantha Russo

Figure 15.6

Miranda Crowell

One of the most important hair coverings was the coif, a cap of white linen or decorative fabric. Hair coif shapes varied from round to heart shaped (gabled).

The veil she wears is known as a "conch". These were sometimes attached at the head and other times at the shoulder. They can reach as far as floor length (Figure 15.7).

The three-masted merchant ship of the East India Company was an impressive sight against the cold sky. The hive of activity on the docks consisted of men in leather jerkins and breeches with shirt sleeves rolled up, who seemed impervious to the cold. Even in their common clothing with embellishments from various continents, with cutless swords at their sides, they moved like a practiced team unloading cargo from the ship (Figure 15.8).

Rae and the Master Merchant stood out against the crowd. The Master Merchant cut an interesting silhouette with his peascod belly and pumpkin trunk hose. He wore a double and ruff collar on his linen shirt and completed his attire with fine leather gloves and shiny buckle shoes below his hose. At his side was a shiny rapier with the emblem of the East India Trading Company. He tipped his hat and inclined his head as Chaney approached (Figure 15.9).

Men's shirts were made of linen and gathered into a round or square neckline with embroidery, cutwork, falling collars, and ruffs.

The peascod belly of Henry the VIII was in fashion.

Rae paid little attention to his sister, as he was involved in some kind of controversy with the Master Merchant over the documents in his hand and the boxes at which he wildly gesticulated his finger.

Figure 15.7

Andrew Tran

15. Northern Renaissance (AD 1500–1600)

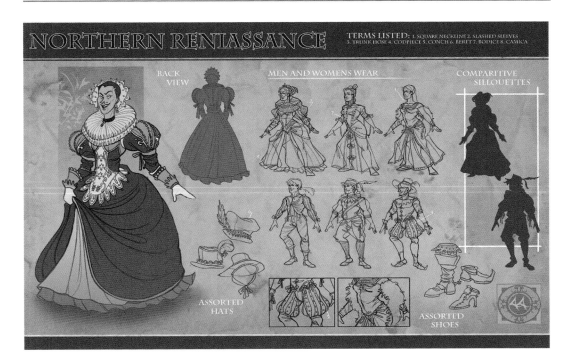

Figure 15.8

Amber Ansdell

Figure 15.9

Madison Swain

Rae looked dashing in his matching jerkin and breeches with covered buttons running up the leg. The fabric reflected the light with the silver thread that was woven into it. His falling collar was pulled out over his cape, which seemed to float off his shoulders in the wind. Under his jerkin the slashing in his doublet showed one of his many brilliant silk undershirts reminiscent of his time in Italy (Figure 15.10).

His thigh-high boots that were wider at the top seemed to be one large cup of lace coming from his breeches. His boots were adorned with leather laplets and spurs. Chaney thought the spurs a bit much, since Rae seldom if ever was on a horse any more. With the sash around his jerkin, he definitely stood out against the mostly black attire of the Dutch (Figure 15.11).

Figure 15.10

Dylan Pock

Figure 15.11

Sebastian Kings

Chaney took a second look at Rae's face that usually revealed a controlled happy man and could see that this was not the best time, so she turned hand headed to her morning appointment. The story would unfold itself soon enough (Figures 15.12 and 15.13).

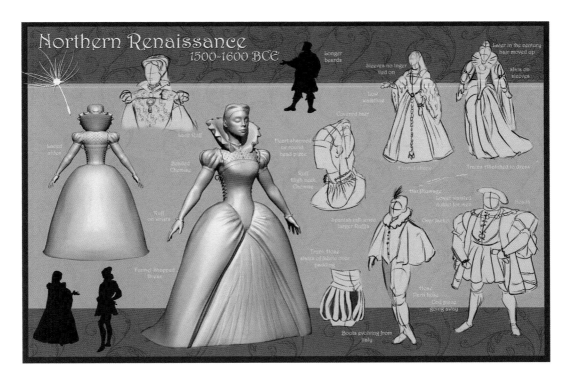

Figure 15.12

Jaime Stagg

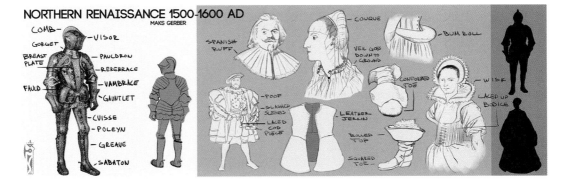

Figure 15.13

Max Gerber

MATERIALS

- Linen
- Lace
- Leather
- Wool
  - Warm + water repellent
- Silk
  - Worn by wealthy
- Brocade
  - Fine, decorative weaving
  - Done with silks, gold, or silver
- Ostrich feathers
  - Worn on hats
- Velvet
  - Black is super high class
- Fur
  - Could be on the sleeves, for instance, a gown
- Necklines
  - Square
  - V-neck
  - High, with large collar
- Silhouette
  - Tight ridged, with poofy slashed sleeves
  - Large collars
  - Exaggerated hips
  - Mutton sleeves (bugle shapes)
  - Large square silhouettes
- Colors
  - Red is a very popular color

The Renaissance color palette also featured *realgar* and among the blues *azurite, ultramarine* and *indigo*. The greens were *verdigris, green earth,* and *malachite*; the yellows were Naples yellow, *orpiment,* and *lead-tin yellow*. Renaissance browns were obtained from umber. Whites were *lead white*, gypsum, and *lime white*, and blacks were *carbon black* and *bone black*.

MEN

Clothing
- Stockings/hosa/hose
  - Tights
  - Multiple layers
- Trunk hose
  - Balloonish breeches
  - Pumpkin hose
  - Stuffing bombast

- Codpiece
  - Triangle of fabric worn over trunk hose
- Camica/chemise
- Peascod belly
  - Popular for a time
  - Padding underneath clothing, aka goosebelly
  - Horsehair/linen
- Doublet
  - Male version of a bodice (tight + ridged)
- Jerkin
  - Usually a sleeveless jacket
- Zipone
  - Belted tunic worn over the knee
- Ruff
  - Men's eventually went unstarched

Headgear/Hair
- Turban
- Short hat with feather
- Short hats resembling a crown (beret)

WOMEN

Clothing
- Camica/Chemise
  - Thin white undergarment made of linen
  - Loose
  - Ruff
- Farthingale
  - Rigid cone-shaped underskirt
  - Whale bone or metal hoops
  - Drumroll (French)
  - Cone (Spanish)
- Kirtle/underskirt/petticoat
  - Underskirt just as elaborate
  - Occasionally has straps
  - Tighter sleeves
- Bumroll
  - Underneath dress for padding
- Gown/dress
  - Bodice (upper ridged part)
  - Large, furlined
  - Detachable sleeves
- Corset
  - Tight bodice
  - During this time had low V-shapes
- Mantle
  - Cloak
  - Furlined if rich

- Ruff
  - Lacey
  - Supportasse (structure)
- Wisk
  - Solid starched lace
  - Heart shaped

Headgear/Hair

Women's hair is usually covered

- Crowns + headbands (conch)
  - With round heart shaped and veil
  - Hair goes up higher
- Turban
- Veils
- Coif
  - Braids wrapped around head

Shoes

- Rounded tops
- Chopine (worn by women)
- Tall shoes, go over shoes
- Clogs

Index

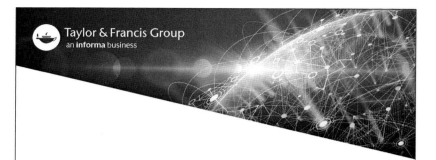